GOD GIVES

THE

INCREASE

by

Gladys   Reifel

"So then neither is he that
planteth   anything,
neither he that watereth;
but God that giveth the increase."
1 Cor. 3:7

Scripture quotations in this book are from the King
James Version of the Holy Bible.

Copyright © 1992
Bethel Publishing Company
1819 South Main Street
Elkhart, IN 46516

All Rights Reserved
ISBN 0-934998-45-0

Edited by Grace Pettifor

Printed in the United States of America

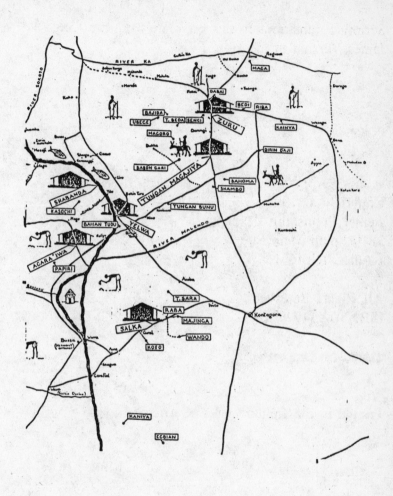

MAP OF OUR AREA OF AFRICA

TABLE OF CONTENTS

PREFACE

In April, 1989, the Michigan District of the Missionary Church asked that a story of Arthur and Gladys Reifel's life and work in Nigeria be written. Art and Gladys responded that they were not writers and could not write a book. Therefore the Conference called for a volunteer to write it.

Linda Duncan, a pastor's wife and student in Journalism, began the project. She spent many hours in research - interviewing the Reifels and others, writing letters to friends and co-workers of the Reifels, and putting it all together in a series of vignettes. For someone who had not lived the story to put it into chronological order was a very difficult task.

Again Art and Gladys were asked to write the story of how God had given the increase in their area of Nigeria. The author undertook the task trusting God for inspiration and guidance. He deserves the honor and praise for what was accomplished through His obedient servants during forty years of missionary service. May others, especially young people, be challenged to wholly follow the Lord in love and obedience to His will.

Many other stories, missionaries, and national Christians have been omitted due to lack of space. The Reifels have retired from active missionary service but the work continues through the ministry of others who are serving Christ.

What a day of rejoicing it will be when those who have prayed, those who have given and those who have gone will all join the Christians from Nigeria who stand before God redeemed because His servants were obedient in gathering in the harvest.

Gladys Reifel

PART I

"PASTO, PASTO, WILL YOU HELP US FIND THE JESUS WAY?"

"Pasto, Pasto, will you help us find the Jesus way?" cried a number of men who had searched the town to find Pastor Ibrahim.

A few weeks before, a fight in the fetish group had caused one group of men to leave. The fetish was the traditional religion of the Kamberi (pronounced COME-burr-i) people. From childhood they had been taught that the fetish was God's way for the Kamberi people to get to heaven. Now they had no way to get to heaven. They were very troubled! What could they do? Prompted by the Holy Spirit, one man ventured his opinion, stating, "We have had white people in this town for a long time who have been telling us about the Jesus way. Some of us agree privately that this is the right way, so why not take it? Let's go the Jesus way!" Immediately they sought out the Christian Pastor to point them to the Jesus way.

Before I tell the rest of the story, let's go back and see how God worked in Salka town long before this incident took place.

* * *

THE FINAL DECISION

Early in our last semester at Fort Wayne Bible Institute, we (Arthur Reifel and I, Gladys Chapman,) received a letter from Rev. R. P. Ditmer informing us that Rev. J. S. Wood, Chairman of the Mission Board, reported that we were recommended by the Michigan Conference Mission Board as applicants for foreign missionary service. As General Secretary, Rev. Ditmer welcomed us and hoped we would pass the examination and meet the requirements of the board. Enclosed were forms to be returned before the board meeting in May.

The next letter we received from the Chairman of the Board was in April stating that the Mission Board Meeting would be in Ohio on May 23. Graduation was scheduled for May 25, two days later. He said, *We will meet applicants in the morning so that you can return in time for the alumni banquet that evening.* We were glad exams were finished.

Another couple and a single lady from the school were also applying to the Mission Board. All five of us traveled to the board meeting together with similar thoughts, wondering what the results of the trip would be. We were all trusting the Lord to lead us and work things out according to His will.

A long rectangular table surrounded by official-looking board members greeted us. After preliminaries, Art and I were interviewed and excused.

As we waited for the others to be interviewed, my thoughts drifted back to the little Mizpah Church in Cass City, Michigan. During revival services, as I was standing at the back of the church, it seemed that an audible voice spoke to me saying, "Gladys, will you go to Nigeria for me?" I looked around but saw no one. Though only eleven, I recognized that voice. After I tossed and turned sleeplessly that night, I called my mother, Mrs. Elmer Chapman.

"Mother," I cried, "I think God wants me to go to Nigeria."

Mother's answer was, "That's fine. Just tell Him, *Yes*, you will go."

I replied, "But I can't leave you and daddy."

As mother knelt by my bed, she was learning to understand the relinquishing love of the Father. Mother explained that God would not require me to go anywhere until I had finished my schooling. I slept easier the rest of the night.

While Art waited, he remembered his wonderful conversion experience at the Christian and Missionary Alliance Church in Cleveland, Ohio, the trip to Fort Wayne Bible Institute, his work in street evangelism, the financial struggles, and his work at the dairy. He recalled his mother's sacrifice of her small inheritance to pay off his final school debt. Graduation was near but he would not receive a diploma until the debt was paid. Gratefully he thanked God for His sustaining power and for Gladys and her encouragement. He knew that all of this was God's plan.

Art anguished inside as he thought of his German Lutheran upbringing and his father who did not approve of his adventurous dream of traveling to Africa to tell the tribes of Nigeria of the Savior. There was an interior decorating business to run and his father felt that Art should have a trade.

After the interviews, the candidates waited impatiently for the Mission Board's decision. By May 26, the decisions were made.

When the letter came, Art held it in his hand. Would it bring good news or bad? "Should I open it right now or wait?" was Art's thought. "Will I be disappointed?" He was unable to delay hearing the final decision so he opened the letter. It read:

This letter is to inform you that you and Gladys have been accepted by the Board as missionaries and are assigned to Nigeria, West Africa. No doubt this will be good news to you and now you can begin to plan, and make your preparations for going.

Due to the fact that you are soon to be married, we will not take any steps to secure your passports until after that event. To do so would involve technical difficulties for Gladys because of the change of name. Please advise me as to the date of your wedding and also your plans for the immediate thereafter so that I will know how to proceed.

Will you please share the contents of this letter with Gladys? [Signed by Rev. R.P. Ditmer]

We were officially approved and could pursue God's call. Our August wedding was changed to June 2 so the passport and visa could be applied for in my married name.

We now had months of extensive preparation ahead of us. Communications from the General Secretary informed us of lists of articles we should take, inoculations we should have, deputational services for which we were to speak, and many other responsibilities to be taken care of before leaving the States.

The *Missionary Banner* stated: *On Tuesday, October 16, 1945, a party of five boarded the Gripsholm and started their journey to Nigeria. By ship they traveled to Alexandria, Egypt, and then by rail and air to Jebba, Nigeria. Those traveling were new missionaries Arthur and Gladys Reifel, Miss Viola Bailey, and Miss Edna Pridham and Miss Luella Reinhart, a second term missionary.*

Each one had their desires, goals and expectations for the future. Arthur Reifel's heart burned with a desire to see the heathen converted. As a bride of four months heading for the tropics of Africa, I was thankful to be accompanied by my husband and companion in life and ministry.

During the weeks of travel, there was time to reflect upon our lives thus far. Art's mind shifted to thoughts of his German Lutheran home and his stern father who expected his children to follow the religion of his family. Art did not learn of a personal relationship with Jesus, who grants forgiveness to those who repent, until after he had quit school in the eighth grade. He realized that God had taken an unmotivated young man and enabled him to finish Bible School and a four-year course at Fort Wayne Bible Institute while working at a dairy to pay his way through school. No financial help came from his father who disapproved of Art's plans and didn't understand his dreams. It was no small struggle for Art to go against his father's wishes concerning college and now, to be leaving for Nigeria. Art's mother had given some approval just before he left for college. While Art was in the process of agonizing over God's call and his father's will, his mother had said, "Art, do what God wants you to do." Those words echoed in his mind as the ship rocked and swayed across the ocean.

Contentment filled Art's heart and mind as he recalled how he had received the knowledge and experience of the Holy Life and infilling of the Holy Spirit at Fort Wayne which had directed his attention to foreign fields of service. On the Practical Work Committee he was assigned tract distribution, a foretaste of his future work, evangelism. During his training, he distributed over 14,000 tracts and personally dealt with one hundred fifty-six people in relation to salvation. Art loved to speak to individuals on a one-to-one basis, and was anticipating this in Nigeria. God had called lean and wiry Art and planted him at Fort Wayne Bible Institute with no high school diploma, no money and no parental approval. Art's aim was high and his call was sure and God was faithful.

With the assurance in my heart that we were headed in the right direction, I thought of the time Miss Hollenbeck visited our home during her furlough when I was five or six years old. As she was getting ready to leave she said to me, "Come spend a weekend with me in Nigeria." I was now going to Nigeria and could accept that invitation.

From the time I was eleven, I had assumed that I would board the ship to Nigeria as a single missionary in the footsteps of a dear family friend, Miss Isabel Hollenbeck. However, as my friendship with Art developed, we began to share a common goal. Art felt called to missionary work in Africa but not to any particular country and I was called to Nigeria. Ours was a God-given relationship, a union where two minds and two spirits desired to serve the Lord. Two lives, one love and a common goal were what we shared. My parents were relieved that I was going to have someone who cared for me to share my life and work in far-off Africa. In those days travel was slow and mail was exceedingly slow but I was not there alone.

Another memory I had was the struggle I had to say a definite *Yes* to the Lord when he asked me to go to Nigeria. My first thoughts had not been of snakes, scorpions, wild animals, bugs and bats but of leaving a close-knit family for several years. Mother had encouraged me to say *Yes* to Jesus and said it would be easier to say goodbye when I was grown up, finished with school and Bible School, and had completed the necessary preparations. The struggle continued for two years. At church I could not sing the song, "I'll go where you want me to go, Dear Lord." I was holding back and had not really yielded except to say, "Yes, Lord, I will go but I hope I do not have to."

At Brown City Camp, when I was thirteen, God continued to speak to me and I asked a woman from my home church, the Mizpah Church of Cass City, Michigan, if she would pray with me. We walked into the woods behind the tabernacle and I said the final and complete *Yes* to the Lord. From then on the mission field was my goal in life. When I graduated from high school, someone offered to pay my way to Business College but I refused because my desire was to go to Bible School. Had it not been for the call of the Lord upon my life, Business College would have been my choice.

Art's poem, <u>Unheeded,</u> reveals the heart's burden that motivated and prepared us for the mud and plaster thatched-roof hut awaiting us in Nigeria.

UNHEEDED

With hearts that are broken, burdened within,
Millions are dying, lost in their sin.
They are searching for truth.
Will their cries go unheeded?
Can the church just stand by
And deny them the Word?
Must they still pray to false gods
And worship in fear,
While the church - like these idols -
Seems not to hear?

Are God's people too busy
To have much concern?
Is there no more desire
Over lost souls to yearn?
Their cries must be answered
From heaven above!
God help us to take them
The Gospel of love.

TROUBLE ON THE GRIPSHOLM

As we continued our journey there was warning of engine trouble on the Gripsholm. The passengers, including about two hundred missionaries, were not worried as they were trusting the Lord for a safe journey. The ship's mechanic said it could probably be fixed in Naples. However, repairs had to be ordered from Sweden since it was a Swedish ship so the delay would be longer than first expected. After sitting in the bay in Naples for two days, we were instructed to board the S.S. General Meigs, an American troop transport, which was heading for Alexandria, Egypt. Although not as comfortable as the passenger ship, we were glad to be moving again. The scenery on the Mediterranean Sea was beautiful. The sunsets were picturesque. Sometimes the water was as smooth as glass but we were reminded of the shipwreck that the Apostle Paul encountered on this very sea.

In four days we arrived in Port Said, Egypt, and were unloaded in the harbor with people being taken to shore in small boats and their baggage carried in on barges. The luggage was all dumped in a huge pile in the center of a large room. Everyone had to sort out their own things. What confusion and scrambling there was as several hundred passengers claimed their belongings.

Art and I found our luggage and went through customs. Art went back to help the other ladies through customs but was not allowed to re-enter the building.

As we sat on our suitcases waiting for the others, we had our first experience with the hot African sun. There was no shade at all. Water sellers were roaming the streets, carrying water in goatskins along with a tin cup so thirsty pedestrians could have a drink. Art and I were very, very thirsty but did not dare take a drink because we had been told that all water must be boiled and cooled because of the frequency of dysentery and other diseases prevalent in Africa. Beggars and non-beggars stuck out their hands for a 'dash' (a small gift of money). As we sat in the heat on our suitcases I began to feel that these people were repulsive and unlovable. Then I remembered all the years I had looked forward to teaching these people about Jesus' love. How could

I ever reach them for Jesus if I allowed this attitude to take root in my heart? Right there outside the customs house door, I asked God to give me a love for the Africans. I wanted to be useful to Him in the work He had called me to do.

When the other three ladies were through customs, the five of us took taxis to the Hotel De La Post. After having lunch, a rest and dinner in our hotel, we gathered in our room. Each one of us drew a promise from a promise box. My promise was from Jeremiah 33:3, "Call unto me, and I will answer thee, and shew thee great and mighty things, which thou knowest not." God was beginning to answer my prayer, and the assurance of His presence was with all five of us as we waited in Egypt. The next day we went to Cairo by train.

NIGERIA AT LAST - KANO, JEBBA

After spending six weeks in Egypt and four days in Palestine, we boarded a British Overseas Airways plane for Kano, Nigeria. What excitement we felt as the plane took off about 3:00 A.M. on December 10. We were served breakfast on the plane and a short time later we arrived in Khartoum in the Sudan. We had a couple hours there and visited the Sudan Interior Mission Headquarters where we were served breakfast again. Lunch was packed by British Airways and put under our seats in the plane. The lunches were eaten before we arrived at a British Airbase in the desert that afternoon. As we walked from the plane to the Airbase building, the sun was so hot that it nearly burned our feet through our shoes.

After dinner that evening most of the passengers retired early. Those who had eaten the lunch under their seats became very ill during the night. Art had a very difficult time with food poisoning but the next morning, by leaning on me, he made his way to the plane for the last lap of the trip. We arrived in Kano, Nigeria, lacking just five days of being two months since we had left the United States.

Our arrival in Nigeria was dampened somewhat when a very weak Art was put to bed for a couple of days by the doctor in Kano. By December 13, when the train was going down country, he made the trip along with the rest of the group. He regrets that he was not a gentleman because he rode to the train station in the car while the women walked.

In Jebba we were met by Miss Isabel Hollenbeck. My first weekend and my first Christmas in Nigeria were spent with Miss Hollenbeck (Holly to us) and the invitation which had been given nearly eighteen years before was kept.

While we were traveling, there were a few questions in our minds, such as, "Where will we be stationed? What will our house be like? Will there be any furniture? Or where will we get some furniture?"

Since part of our trip was by air we could take only forty-four pounds each in our suitcases, so we had very little with which to begin life in Africa. Our boxes and trunks would follow later.

While we were wondering where we would be stationed it seemed that God kept impressing the word 'Salka' on our minds. So it came as no surprise to us when we reached Jebba and the Field Superintendent,

Rev. Russell Sloat, told us that we were stationed in Salka. We were assured in our hearts that this was God's leading, and that we were in the center of God's will for us. It brought us real peace to know that whatever was before us, we were surrounded by His love and care.

During the month that Art and I were in Jebba, the mission headquarters, we began to get oriented to the country and to the work. Since we were to learn the Hausa language, we began language study immediately so we could at least say 'Hello' to the people in Salka when we arrived.

Christmas Day, 1945, was our first Christmas in Nigeria, our first Christmas as a married couple, and our first Christmas away from our families in America. Were we lonesome or homesick? No, not really, although we missed them. It was a joy to celebrate Jesus' birth with our new brothers and sisters in Christ.

After a worship service in the forenoon, the missionaries had a Christmas party for their staff and teachers at the school in the afternoon. They played games, sang Christmas Carols and served snacks. The day after Christmas, (Boxing Day in British Territory), was also a holiday and the missionaries celebrated their Christmas that day. We had drawn names to get each other gifts so we had a gift exchange and a real Christmas dinner. In the gift exchange Art got a bottle of StaWay (a deodorant), a watch band, a candy bar and a stick of gum. I received a small dyed calabash, a bar of soap, a hankie, a crochet hook, a candy bar, a stick of gum and three safety pins.

After New Year's Day, Rev. Sloat was going to

Igbetti before he took us up country. He asked Art to go along. They planned to stay overnight. Miss Anderson had a chicken that she said the cook could kill and fix for their supper. The cook killed the chicken but did not have any oil to cook it in. Rev. Sloat gave him some money to go to market and get the oil. When the chicken was brought to the table it looked so good but was it hot! This was Art's first experience with Nigerian hot peppers. The peppers were in the oil the cook had bought at the market. Rev. Sloat did not have much drinking water that night as Art drank most of it before it was even cooled after having been boiled.

SALKA - THE TRIP, HISTORY, SETTLING IN

On January 19, 1946, Rev. Sloat, Art and I began our trip to Salka which was about one hundred fifty miles from Jebba. We made a short stop at Mokwa, another one of the mission stations. A few miles from there we turned north, leaving the main road to Kontagora and northern Nigeria, to follow a shortcut to Kontagora that had been made through the bush by army trucks during World War II. There were very few villages along the way. About halfway there the Model A in which we were traveling stopped. After trying to get it going without any success, Rev. Sloat asked Art and I to stay with the car and he would try to get help. Our thoughts were, "Where is he going to get help in the bush like this? What kind of help is he looking for? What do the Nigerians know about cars when they have none?"

While he was gone some people came along the path and wanted to know the trouble. They jabbered to Art and I in a language we had never heard until we arrived in Africa. We tried to use a few words we knew to tell them that a man had gone seeking help but we never knew if we got our point across. We had some real misgivings about being left alone in the bush, not knowing where we were, nor where Rev. Sloat had gone. Were there wild animals around? Were these Nigerians hostile or friendly to the missionaries? We knew the Lord was with us and our trust was in Him.

About three hours later, Rev. Sloat returned and got the car running and we were on our way again. With no more car trouble the remainder of the trip, we arrived in Salka on a pitch black Saturday night.

On the continent of Africa, in the country of Nigeria, in a little village was a backward tribe called the Kamberi. They were steeped in tradition and busy with domestic life; hunting, farming, grinding grain between stones, carrying babies on their backs, and calabashes on their shoulders.

Their religion involved sacrificing animal blood, seeking the help of the spirits to bless them, which kept them (especially the women) in fear and subjection. It was a religion of male dominance. Though religion was restricted to the men, all were involved in the rituals of blood sacrifices of chickens to receive help from the spirit world. No woman had ever dared to see the fearsome fetish dragon, Magiro. If she were to see the dragon there would be much pain and suffering and death. For generations they had accepted this religion. The men enjoyed the superiority it gave them, and the license to sit and absorb the guttural sounds of their elders in the bush traditon, becoming drunk on the beer the women were ordered to make.

We wanted to bring the message that all help comes from the Lord Jesus, if they would repent and let Christ lead them. They were slow to accept the message brought to them by the missionaries.

In the early 1920's Rev. Ira Sherk, the Nigerian Field Director, and Rev. Joseph Ummel began to scout around to find a place for a mission station in Northern Nigeria. In the first area they tried, they woke up in the morning to find themselves surrounded by water. They decided to try another area which turned out to be Salka.

Mrs. Mabel Ummel states that on January 23, 1923, Joseph Ummel left from Jebba for this newly chosen spot in Salka with forty-one men carrying loads on their heads. Averaging about nineteen miles a day, they reached Salka on January 31, 1923. In November, 1924, Paul Ummel, Joseph's brother, and the Durkees arrived to help with the work. Later the Durkees carried on in Salka and the Ummels moved further north to open another station.

From Rev. Joseph Ummel's tiny seed in 1923 through a chain of missionaries until 1943, there had been consistent missionary involvement in Salka. For two years prior to our arrival, there had been no missionary representation. As we learned of the previous years of missionary work there, we realized that perseverance was needed in the task to which we were called. Our success lies in God's timing. It is shared with the pioneers who went before us, with brothers and sisters who prayed, and with those who have stood with us throughout the years of our missionary service.

"And he that reapeth receiveth wages, and gathereth

fruit unto life eternal: that both he that soweth and he that reapeth may rejoice together. And herein is that saying true, One soweth, and another reapeth. I sent you to reap that whereon ye bestowed no labour: other men laboured, and ye are entered into their labours'' (John 4:36-38).

Having arrived in Salka on a pitch dark night, we had seen very little of the town of Salka or the house in which we were going to live. Rev. Sloat unlocked the door of our house and we entered a very large building. There were no lights to turn on. A small kerosene lamp on the table was ready to light. To our eyes, which were used to electricity, it seemed like only the light of a small candle.

The house measured about forty by seventy-two feet and was divided into three rooms; a dining room, a living room and a bedroom surrounded by a nine-foot wide veranda. There were no ceilings but plenty of bats! The kitchen was a small building behind the house with a galvanized metal roof. Thatched roofs are not very fireproof.

There was some furniture in the house, much of it homemade. We entered this house with joy and great anticipation as this was where we were going to set up housekeeping. From the time we were married until we left for Nigeria four months later, we had lived with my parents so had not set up housekeeping in America. It was our first home! We had great expectations that God was going to bless our ministry and use us to stand in the gap and reach the Kamberi people for the Lord.

STAND IN THE GAP
by Art Reifel

We cannot deny the truth of God's Word;
There are millions of souls who never have heard;
Without Christ they are facing eternal Hell,
While we are reluctant the story to tell.

We know they are wandering in darkness and gloom
With no hope of escaping eternal doom.
Our love has grown cold-we heed not their plight-
Forgetting that all are the same in His sight.

We lack the compassion, our vision is dim
Because our lives are not centered in Him.
He set the example, then told us to go.
He helps in the reaping if we will but sow.

We stand in the gap; we can earnestly pray
And ask Him to lead us each step of the way.
Our love will increase and the vision be clear,
We will seek the lost sheep that to Him are so dear.

MEETING THE KAMBERI

Our first day in Salka was a Sunday. The small church in town had morning and evening services which we attended. The services were in the Hausa or Kamberi languages so we did not understand a thing. No one in Salka or the nearby villages understood or spoke English. During the afternoon we walked around the town with Rev. Sloat. He introduced us to the Chief and some of the people of the town. The population was about two thousand. We were also introduced to some of the customs of the people and the darkness and hopelessness in which the people lived.

One of the first things we saw was the offerings that

had been made to appease the evil spirits. Small calabashes of grain, peanuts, an egg, and bolls of cotton
were placed in a fork in the path for the spirits. Another
path detoured around the fetish hut where the dragon of
the Magiro fetish was said to live. No one went near
that hut except the leader and older men who were
followers of the fetish. On the doorposts of the entrance
huts of each compound were the blood and feathers of
chickens to induce the spirits to give them a good
harvest from their farms, good health and prosperity.
These things made a real and lasting impression on our
minds.

Their style of living was interesting to us also. The
Kamberi people all lived in town and walked out to
their farms every day. In the town whole families lived
in the same compound. Grandpa was at the head with
all the sons and grandsons living in the same enclosure
surrounded by mud walls or fences made of grass mats
or cornstalks. When a daughter got married she went to
live in her husband's compound. When a son got
married he brought his wife or wives home to the
family compound. Each wife had her own hut so there
were many round mud huts in the compounds.

Running through the center of town was a stream
which was their water supply. It was supplied by a
spring in the rocks. The sheep, goats and donkeys all
drank from this stream. The townspeople took their
baths and washed their clothes in the stream. The
women and girls washed their dishes (calabashes) and
cooking pots there, and then filled the large calabashes
with water to take home and cook their food.

The food was made from grain, either guinea corn or

millet, which was ground into flour by rubbing two stones together with the grain between them. The ground grain was made into a very thick porridge which could be taken with their fingers and dipped into the bowl of gravy made from meat, vegetables or leaves of certain trees. Usually it was made from vegetables or leaves because meat was very scarce. The women cooked the food, then the men sat down in groups to eat. The women ate in their groups but never with the men. The menu was the same for two or three meals a day every day. If they did not have the porridge, they thought they had not eaten.

Tribal marks were something we had not seen before going to Africa. The Kamberi tribal mark was one long scar on each cheek. These were put into the faces of children when they were small by making a long cut with a sharp knife or razor blade in each cheek. Then a red substance was rubbed into the cut so that it would leave a large scar on the face when it healed. Perhaps this red substance had a little antibiotic in it so the cuts would not get infected.

We visited two lepers that afternoon. One leper woman had been a Christian but had ceased following the Lord when there were no missionaries there to read the Word for her or pray with her. The leper man, Kamashi, was confined to his compound because his feet were only stubs. He was an encouragement to us because he truly loved the Lord.

That afternoon we learned that there were only four Christians among the entire Kamberi tribe of about sixty thousand people. Kamashi, the leper man, and DanDodo, the Chief's son who had been raised by the

Durkees from the time he was nine years old, were the two Christians in Salka. There was also a Christian Kamberi couple who worked for the missionaries in Yelwa, about sixty miles away. DanDodo would prove to be an invaluable help to us and became an influential witness for Christ. He had carried on church services when no missionaries were there and was the cook for Rev. Sloat and us.

When that first Sunday in Salka came to a close we had many new impressions to process and the weight of responsibility was beginning to rest upon us. We knew that Rev. Sloat would soon be returning to his responsibilities in Jebba.

Rev. Sloat told us about the school that was carried on in the evenings. Just as the sun was setting and people were returning from their farms, the school bell would ring. Young men and boys came to school while their mothers went home to prepare the evening meal. He said, "After I leave, you will be continuing the school."

Art looked at him in surprise, "How can we teach school when we can not understand or speak the language?"

Rev. Sloat said, "You will find out tonight."

We found out as we went to school with him the first Monday night that it was not nearly as difficult as we expected. Hausa was relatively easy to read. It was written and spelled as it was spoken and most of the vowels had only one sound (much simpler than English). We soon learned to pronounce the words although we did not know their meaning. From that first Monday night we went to school and taught many to read and write in the Hausa language. Some of the pupils had begun to read their Bibles, some were reading a simple Bible story book, and others were still in their Primers when Rev. Sloat left. We were learning more of the language as we taught.

Before Rev. Sloat returned to Jebba, he engaged Mallam Tanko, a Hausa man who had taught other missionaries the language. Mallam came to the compound every day to help us with language study. He could neither read nor write but he talked to us and helped us with pronunciation as we read to him. Language study became the first priority as we settled into our home and work in Salka.

One afternoon Rev. Sloat took us to a little village three miles from Salka to meet the people and hold a village service. When we arrived in Raba we went to the Chief's compound to greet him and let him know that we wanted to speak to the people. Of course, when people heard the car coming, many children, young men and older ones were curious to see and hear what we wanted. By the time we reached the Chief's entrance hut, quite a crowd was following us. The Chief was not too friendly and really did not show proper respect to his visitors according to their customs. However a service was held and the way of salvation was shared as it had been many times before.

As time went by Art went to that village many times and even began reading classes there. The Chief eventually became friendly and accepted the Savior as well as the missionaries.

Rev. Sloat stayed with us for a month. Finally the day came when he headed south again. We will never forget the day he drove out of our driveway and we were left in Salka - just the two of us to carry on the Lord's work among the Kamberi people.

Art turned to me saying, "I'm glad the Lord never leaves us. We can depend on Him for His help."

I stood there thinking of the big task that was before us - approximately thirty-three thousand people in Auna District of which Salka was only one small town. No other missionaries were working in the district. It looked like an impossible task but God reminded me of the boy who gave his lunch with which Jesus fed the multitude. When Andrew brought that little lunch to Jesus he said, "There is a lad here, which hath five barley loaves, and two small fishes: but what are they among so many?" (John 6:9). Yes, there were just the two of us. What were we among so many? If we were in the Lord's hands as completely as the boy's lunch was, He could use us to bless the multitude too. That was our desire in Kamberi land. God would use our feeble efforts and our meager offering to meet the needs of the people.

THE WORK BEGUN

After our first Easter in Salka we wrote to friends in America saying: *We are now living among this group of people, and truly the darkness is great. The only hope is our living Saviour, but so few know Him . . . The Kamberi have their fetishes, and they do all they can to please the evil spirits so these spirits will not bring them harm, but still they are enslaved by the only one who can destroy their souls in hell-Satan. Often in the evening when we return from school we hear the voice* of what the townspeople say is the evil spirit talking to them. In reality, the evil spirit is only a man talking into the end of a long hollow stick which has sort of a whistle in the other end. It makes a rather weird and screechy noise. They believe with all their hearts that it is a spirit. Only the power of Jesus Christ can set them free, but our God is able to deliver them.

Our present task is learning the Hausa language. We can do so little until we can talk to the people in their own tongue, but God is helping us and we are seeing encouraging signs. We believe the Holy Spirit is definitely speaking to some hearts. Oh, that they would follow His leading. This morning before church our two workmen went to town with us. We took the accordion and played and sang for a leper man and woman. We also had prayer with them. The leper woman had followed the Lord at one time, and this morning when we got up from prayer she had tears in her eyes. We surely wish we could talk to her, but we know God can talk to her in a language she understands.

Along with language study and the nightly school, Art has begun visiting villages in the surrounding area. I am doing some dispensary work. Malaria, dysentery, and ulcers are the physical needs which bring most of the people for help.

On a Sunday afternoon a man from a village came to us wanting medical help. He said that his child had had a bad cold for several days. Upon arriving in the home we could easily see that the trouble was more than a cold and the case was practically hopeless. The child of about three years of age was literally nothing but skin and bones. She would take no nourishment. We tried to give her some medicine and we believe she got a little as she seemed a little bit brighter the next day. We made several visits on Monday, but the end came during the night. Another colored blossom had been picked for Jesus. We could accept that, but the darkness, ignorance, and hopelessness of the people weighs on us. Frustration at our limited language skills adds to that weight.

Another incident which became heavy on our hearts was the death of Tsofo Mai-Wayo. A couple days before his death he brought eggs to the mission compound to sell and we had entered into a conversation (what we could) along spiritual lines. He thought he had plently of time yet to accept the Lord as his Saviour even if he was an old leper man. He put off the day of salvation, not knowing that in two days his life on earth would be finished. Oh, if men and women throughout the world would only realize the peril of saying not today when God says, "Today is the day of salvation." It seems that little visible results have been seen in Salka this past year, but seed has been sown and Gospel light has been spread to dark hearts. Continue to pray that a number who know the way of salvation will no longer delay in coming to the Saviour.

INTERLUDE FOR CONNIE'S ARRIVAL

The rainy season in Nigeria usually begins in April or May and there is only a dry season road to Salka, which is seventeen miles off the main road. It is impossible to travel to Salka by car after July. Rev. Sloat made a visit to Salka in July and I went to Yelwa with him to stay until we went down to the coastal city of Lagos for the arrival of our first child. While in Yelwa, I continued to study language and frequently went to the dispensary to learn from Edma Brubacher who cared for those coming for treatment. Devotions were held in the dispensary every morning before medicine or treatments were given. It was in the Yelwa dispensary that I gave my first devotional talk using the Hausa language. I also prayed my first prayer in Hausa in July, 1946, six months after arriving in Salka.

I also helped Mrs. Brubacher with the delivery of a baby. I was very grateful for that opportunity as I delivered many babies after that time during our years in Nigeria.

Art and I left Yelwa at the end of August to go to Lagos. It was several weeks before the baby was expected but we had to travel several hundred miles and could not wait until the last minute.

On October 8, 1946, little Connie Marie made her appearance. The long days of waiting were over and we began to look forward to the trip back home to Salka. Several things had happened up country during the weeks we were away. While in Lagos we heard that the Chief of Salka had passed away. Russell Sloat and Evelyn Kress were married in Share. The Annual Field Conference had been held and we were anxious to hear the reports and decisions that had been made during the Conference.

After we arrived back in Jebba by train, we heard that we were stationed in Yelwa for the coming year. That meant going back to Salka to pack up our things and move. However things did not work out that way. Although part of our things were moved, they were brought back to Salka and unpacked there.

We had wanted to ask the Field Board at Conference to send another missionary to Salka to help with the medical work. Instead there was discussion about closing the station in Salka because of the lack of response to the Gospel message. Missionary work had been carried on there for twenty-three years and still there were only a few Christians. God saw the future and loved the Kamberi people, so He put it in the hearts of the majority to keep it open and the station was not closed. Another missionary, Viola Bayly, (now Mrs. Charles Nelson), was sent to Salka to do dispensary work. She traveled with us on the train to Zungeru when we returned from Lagos. Rev. Paul Ummel was in Zungeru to meet us when the train arrived so we did not have a long truck ride to get back home. What a blessing with a new baby on board.

BEGINNING TO SEE FRUIT

During our first year in Salka one young man, the gardener on the mission compound, accepted Christ as his Savior. Even one soul is worth more than the whole world. See Matthew 16:26. Some time later Miss Bayly (Mrs. Nelson) wrote a letter which was printed in the *Missionary Banner* in 1947. She wrote: *This last week our hearts have rejoiced as four young men from the school stepped out for God. One evening two of them came out to the compound and told us that their hearts agreed and they wanted to repent. How we did rejoice. They were so happy. The darkness had passed away and the Light of the World had entered into their hearts. One of the young men held up his lantern and* said, "Why, I've got a light in my heart like this!" Two nights later two more young men came out to tell us that they, too, wanted to repent.

One of these young men has had quite a difficult time of late. His father was very angry when he heard that he had become a Christian. His family hid his books and Bible and then threatened to burn them. But he came to school anyway. The next day his father went to the bush and prepared a whip, then came home threatening to kill the young man. Again he managed to get away and come to school. After school he feared to go home but we tried to encourage him and tell him that God would go with him and protect him. Feeling very much burdened for him, we had a season of prayer as soon as we arrived home and committed him to the Lord. The next day he told us that his father and ten men came to him and all of them said they were going to beat him. But he said nothing happened. God stayed their hands and soon they walked off and left him. They are still persecuting him some but they are afraid to say or do very much. God can cause the wrath of man to praise Him and He has surely done it here. This morning a man from this young man's compound came to church. I have never seen him in church before and I believe it is partly due to this young man's testimony.

BAWA DANIYA BORN

Daniya and his wife, Asulu, were two of the four Christians in the Kamberi tribe when we arrived in Salka. At that time they lived in Yelwa and Daniya was working for the Honsbergers. When they went home for furlough, Daniya came back to Salka to work for us.

We were happy to have someone who had already been trained to work for white people. Sometimes it is very frustrating to both the white people and the Nigerians who are learning to work for them. Our customs and our homes are very different from theirs. The nationals experience culture shock when they enter a white person's home to work, just as the missionary passes through culture shock in adapting to the land of his calling. Everything must be neat and clean. Dishes - WOW! What do they do with all those dishes? When they are going to eat, each piece of silverware must be put in the right place on the table, and the right size plate must be used. The dishes must then all be washed and scalded before drying. Beds must be made! They do not simply pick up their mats and roll them up until nighttime again. The sheets must be straight on the bed and wrinkle free. How complicated their life is! Fingers were made before forks. Men slept on the floor before beds were invented-and the list could go on for the adjustments they have to make to work for white people.

Daniya had already passed through all of this so he helped me with the cleaning, washing dishes and sometimes caring for Connie, whom they called Talata because she was born on Tuesday. Having his help freed me a considerable amount of time so I could do more studying and visiting.

Soon Daniya's wife became pregnant. They were happy because they had no children, but also sad because she had lost six babies. Some were lost during the early months of pregnancy and some were near full-time. There were no doctors or midwives nearby where she could get more help than could be given at the mission dispensaries. Although Viola Bayly had been doing the dispensary work in Salka for a few months, she was away when it came time for the baby to arrive. I was called upon to deliver the baby. How thankful I was for the little experience I received while in Yelwa. I had also given birth myself, which was a real help in knowing what to expect and what to do. Still it was with great fear and trembling that I went to the dispensary to deliver this little one all by myself. I was thinking not only of the process of delivery, but also of all the trouble and opposition Daniya and Asulu had faced because of the babies she had lost. Their people had told them that the reason their babies died was because they were following the white man's God and the spirits were angry with them. Asulu's folks had tried to get her to leave Daniya and marry someone else so she would have a living baby. Daniya's folks were telling him to take another wife and he would have some children. The pressure on them was great and would be greater still if this baby died too. They had stood true to the Lord thus far but, if this one died, would the pressure on them be too great? Would they listen to what their folks were telling them? What kind of ridicule and opposition would they face if they had to bury this baby too?

Therefore my concern was not just for the delivery of this baby, but also for this Christian couple, the only one in the entire Kamberi tribe. I called upon the Lord Jesus who loved this couple more than I did because He gave His life for them. The Lord just reminded me that the help I could give Asulu was much better than she could have gotten in town. He calmed my fears and my trembling ceased.

A strong, healthy baby boy was born, and given the name 'Bawa' which means 'a servant.' Daniya and Asulu had a living baby boy. God answered prayer and gave help in time of need. They had five more children after this - three boys and two girls. Asulu never left Daniya to marry another man and Daniya never took a second wife.

Daniya was a deacon in the Salka church when he died at Christmastime in 1989. He had been used of the Lord to help many people both physically and spiritually, as he worked at the hospital at Tungam Magajiya and at the Dispensary at Zuru for many years.

OUR FIRST LANGUAGE EXAM

It was the rule of the U.M.C.A. Mission in Nigeria that new missionaries learn the language of the people in the area where they were to work. After about eighteen months on the field they were given an exam to see how they were progressing. After about three years, before furlough, they were to write the second exam. If they did not pass the language exams, they could be asked not to return to the field after furlough.

Mrs. Edma Brubacher, who had become very proficient in the Hausa language, gave Miss Bayly and us our first exam. All three of us passed with fairly good grades. We really praised the Lord for His help in language study. This encouraged us to study hard for the second exam. About a month after we wrote our first exam, Mallam Tanko, who had been helping us with the language, became ill. Art wrote about his death in the *Missionary Banner* saying: *The Moham-medan died knowing the way but-he died in darkness. Our hearts were made sad this morning by the news of the death of Mallam Tanko. This man has heard the way of Salvation for many years and has admitted to us that he knew that he should repent and follow the Lord. He also knew that he would not get to heaven because of his long Moslem prayers and his good works. The other day when I went to see him after hearing of his illness, I pled with him to accept the blessed Savior. I pointed out to him that this might be his last chance to accept Christ but he paid little attention to the plea. This morning they sent for medicine but before we had the medicine in hand, we heard the weeping and wail-ing and knew that he was beyond our help. He had gone out into a dark eternity.*

Mallam Tanko had worked with several missionaries helping them learn the language. He had the opportu-nity of hearing the Gospel many, many times over a period of a number of years. But he thought there would always be another opportunity to accept Jesus as his Savior before he died. So when he became ill he ex-pected to get better in a few days. When Art was talking to him about accepting Jesus now, he said, "I am not going to die yet." He did not know that he would not be alive in another twenty-four hours. He had rejected the only way that would have brought him eternal peace and joy in God's house forever.

THE LEPER WOMAN LIVES WITH JESUS
On our first Sunday afternoon in Salka with Rev. Sloat, we met a leper woman who had known the Lord

but, since there was no one to read God's Word to her,
she had given up following Him. We visited her frequently and read the Word to her although we could not
talk with her at first because of the language barrier.
One day when we visited her, she crawled out of her hut
and knelt with us in prayer. She asked God to restore
unto her the joy of her salvation. God answered her
prayer and again she walked with Him. She looked
forward to living with Jesus in His heavenly home.

Her body was badly eaten by leprosy. She had no
hands nor feet-just stubs. She was unable to work and
was dependent on others. Her only enjoyment was her
knowledge of the Savior and the joy of knowing that
someday she would no longer be a leper. The last words
we heard her say were, "There'll be no sickness or
trouble there." She lives with Jesus now.

At the Field Conference in 1947, Viola Bayly, Art
and I were stationed back in Salka for our third year.
We went back trusting the Lord to continue to work
with us. Now that we were understanding and speaking
more Hausa, Art began visiting villages more frequently and regularly. He tried systematically to reach
the villages in a twelve-mile radius around Salka,
realizing the advantage of reaching the nearby villages
frequently instead of traveling farther away and only
going once or twice a year. He traveled by walking or
riding a bicycle. During our first term we did not see
much spiritual fruit from this endeavor, but people
grew more friendly as they became acquainted with
him and realized that he cared for them.

EARL'S ARRIVAL

For Christmas, 1947, the missionaries from Zuru, Salka and Yelwa met together in Yelwa to celebrate. After Christmas Connie and I went up to Zuru with Dr. and Mrs. Ross Bell to await the arrival of our second child. Art went back to Salka for a few weeks and then went up to Tungam Magajiya where he helped Mr. Honsberger build the doctors' houses. The Women's Missionary Societies in the United States and Canada were raising money to build a hospital. Dr. and Mrs. Bell were living in Zuru until the houses were built and the hospital was started.

Art helped with the building during the week but came up to Zuru for the weekend. During the night on February 1, 1948, Art went back down to T.M. to get Mrs. Honsberger who was a registered nurse. She came up to Zuru to help Dr. Bell with the delivery and also care for the baby and me. It appeared that the baby was going to arrive a couple weeks early. We were not ready for the occasion. A little round mud hut was to be the delivery room and we knew that it was not prepared. Dr. and Mrs. Bell worked most of the night getting it ready. They moved the kitchen table to the delivery room, collected the necessary supplies and did many other things in preparation for the arrival of the baby. Baby Earl arrived at 7:30 on a cold, windy Monday morning. It really sounded like a February blizzard outside with the heavy wind and dust blowing across the town. When the mail truck came into town that day, they brought the operating table. Earl had arrived a few hours too early to be the first to use the new table.

One morning while I was still in bed, Art and I were having devotions together. I was lying down and Art was kneeling by a chair beside the bed. When we finished praying, Art stood up and looked down and there was a snake around the leg of his chair. We praised the Lord because he saw the snake before the snake bit him.

OUR SECOND LANGUAGE EXAM

After returning to Salka with baby Earl, we knew that it would be time for our second and final language exam soon. We had no teacher to help us after Mallam Tanko died, but we wanted to really concentrate on the language study. Eventually a man from Yelwa came to Salka and worked with Viola, Art and me for two months. It was suggested that we wait until after our furlough to take the second exam since we had no one to help us much after our first exam. All three of us wanted to get it over and finished.

Arrangements were made for us to go to a sister mission for the exam. Toward the end of September, Dr. and Mrs. Bell came to Salka on their return from their vacation in Jos. Mrs. Bell was going to babysit with Connie and Earl while Dr. Bell took Viola, Art and me to Wushishi to write our exam.

We arrived in Wushishi in the late afternoon to be ready for our exam in the morning. When the three of us went to take our exam, the first words from Miss Clark were, "I am giving you our new regular exam."

Our hearts sank! When the Bells were in Jos they had heard that a new exam had been created for this sister mission because they felt the old one was too easy. The news was that no one had passed it from among the twenty-eight who had taken it. The exam was, in fact, *very* difficult. Before we returned to Salka that day Miss Clark told us that we had all passed the oral part. She had not checked the written part yet. We really praised the Lord for that news and we knew that we had done our best whatever the results were. We did all pass the test. After the exam, we went back to Salka to pack up our things.

FURLOUGH TIME

With the exams behind us, we could concentrate on preparing for our first furlough. It was time for Conference and then we were going home. Other missionaries would be living in our house during our time at home so we packed our things back into our boxes. Farewells were said.

Some of the townspeople were very sad because they thought they would not see us again. In the past others had come and gone, so they were not sure we would come back although we told them that if God so willed we would be back.

Dr. Bell had asked if Daniya could come and work at the hospital while we were away, so that there would be a contact for the Kamberi people. He felt that they would be more willing to come to the hospital with their illnesses if there was that contact. So Daniya and family moved to Tungam Magajiya (T.M.) and he worked at the hospital.

Just before the middle of October we left Salka to go to Conference, and then after Conference we would sail for America. The ship we were booked on was to sail in about two weeks. However, our ship left early and booking was made on another ship, the S.S. Templar, which was sailing on November 20. We thanked the Lord for another booking so quickly. That ship stopped in Takoradi and loaded manganese, then headed for New York. After traveling through a severe storm at half speed, we stood on deck watching the New York skyline come into view on the morning of December 23. We were home in time for a family Christmas in 1948!

For missionaries, furlough time is usually a time of much traveling from church to church sharing with people and congregations what God is doing in their particular field of work. It is a time of making new friends and getting reacquainted with former ones. It is a time to visit family and relatives and prepare to return to the field.

During the year we were home, some people began to feel that we should have a vehicle when we returned to Nigeria. We had two small children and lived about a hundred miles from the hospital. What if one of them became ill and we had no way to get to the doctor? The Women's Misssionary Societies in Michigan took on the project of helping us purchase a new Dodge pickup. After its purchase the Mizpah Church had a dedication service for it. We wanted it to be used to bring honor to His name and to be a real help and blessing in furthering His work in Nigeria.

PART II

SETTING FORTH AGAIN

In October, 1949, Art and I and Connie and Earl said goodbye to our loved ones and friends in America and headed for Nigeria again. We drove our new Dodge pick-up to Port Arthur, Texas, where we boarded the S.S. Del Mundo, an American freighter going to West Africa. On this trip we were accompanied by Rev. and Mrs. Willis Hunking going to Nigeria for their first term, and Miss Annie Yeo returning for her third term.

Since the ship was still being loaded, the five of us missionaries went into town on Sunday to go to church. We found the Grace Church of the Nazarene and had a precious time of fellowship with the people there. We were all asked to give our testimonies and they arranged a special missionary service in the afternoon. Miss Yeo was the main speaker and told of her shipwreck experience which had occured on her way home toward the end of World War II.

That morning Connie and Earl were taken to the nursery of the church. Just two weeks afterward, while traveling across the ocean, they both came down with the real red measles. That was not such a bad time for them to have the measles as I did not have anything else to do but to look after them.

As we traveled along on a very calm and smooth sea the words of a song kept going over and over in my mind: "Fear thou not for I am with thee. I will still thy Pilot be." Also the verses: "Be strong and of a good courage; be not afraid, neither be thou dismayed: for the Lord thy God is with thee whithersoever thou goest" (Joshua 1:9). And: "And, behold, I am with thee, and will keep thee in all places whither thou goest, and will bring thee again into this land; for I will not leave thee, until I have done that which I have spoken to thee of" (Genesis 28:15). The promises of God are comforting and assuring. What more could one wish for than knowing that He has promised His continual presence, and will never leave us! We arrived in Lagos on December 2, just two months after we left home.

VICTORIES IN SALKA

After arriving in Salka and getting settled into our home and work I wrote a letter to the folks back home saying: *Nearly two months have already slipped by since we arrived in Salka. Upon our arrival we thanked God for His blessings on the work during our furlough year under the supervision of Miss Eileen Sider and Miss Louise Lorriane. It made our hearts rejoice to see how a few had grown in grace and were becoming strong in the Lord. Soon after our arrival two or three young men came to the compound and told how they had listened to Satan's voice. They confessed their sin and are going on with the Lord.*

Our hearts continue to praise Him because of three who have accepted Christ as their Savior during the past month. Last week the townspeople had their sacrifice of chickens followed by the feast which they have annually about this time. One of these young converts met with much opposition as he refused to offer his chicken and even to eat the meat that others had offered. More than one Christian young man went to bed hungry that night because they refused to eat the meat that had been offered to the spirits and to take part in the fetish feast. Fetish worship no longer has a hold on them since they have been set free by Jesus Christ our Lord.

The second one who came to Christ for forgiveness was a heavy drinker. Many times in the market on Saturday he would get drunk and become the laughingstock of the town. God is helping him and he has not touched beer since his conversion.

The third convert has been hearing the voice of God calling him to repentance for a long time, but he held back because of fear. He knew opposition was ahead if he accepted Christ. We had sent letters home requesting prayer for him. Your prayers have been answered, but continue to pray that each of these three will become strong Christians and real witnesses for Him.

We, and many of you at home have been praying with us, that God would raise up some national workers here in Salka. Last week three of the young men left for Zuru to attend the short-term Bible School under the supervision of Phoebe (Mrs. Paul) Ummel. Two of these have told us that God has very definitely called them into His service. The other one wants to be engaged in Christian work and is following step by step with God until He makes His will known.

One of these three young men, Indazo, has met with

much persecution, to a greater degree than most of the others, ever since his conversion three years ago. Two of the young men left here on Monday morning, but Indazo's father refused to let him go. He even came out to the compound to be sure that he did not go when the mission truck left for Tungam Magajiya; however, that evening Indazo came to our compound and told Art that he was disobeying God's voice if he didn't go and he would have to stand in judgment before God for his sin. Another Christian man, as well as Art and I, advised him to go even against his father's wishes if God was so definitely talking to his heart. The next morning he came out with his little bundle of clothes under his arm and a few minutes later he started out by foot on his way to Zuru, one hundred twenty miles away. A short time later his father came and wanted to know where Indazo was. He was very angry and said he was going to Zuru to force him to come back, but he never went. Others from the compound told him there was no reason for his hindering him because he would be back before the farming season began.

When Indazo returned home, his father was so happy he gave him a bicycle and told him he could use it to go to the villages. At times after this he would still oppose him for a time, but not so severely. As far as we know his father never accepted the Lord as his Savior.

GOD USES THE PICK-UP TRUCK

After we had been back in Salka for some months, Art tells the story of Mindali's conversion to friends in America:

Mindali has been attending school regularly for a

long time. He began to read his Bible about two or three years ago. God has been talking to him about accepting Jesus as his Savior. He wants to be a Christian but was afraid of the opposition he knew he would have to face if he became a Christian; therefore, he kept putting off the day of salvation. In prayer meeting a short time ago, the people were giving testimonies and he told how God had talked to him and led him to make his decision for Christ.

We had been going to Raba every Sunday for services. We took some of the Christian young men to help with the singing, but we found that there were always others who wanted to go for the ride. We were not going for a pleasure trip so we refused to take them. Mindali was frequently among those who were left behind. In his testimony that evening he said that God began to talk to him and tell him that some day he would want to enter heaven and the door would be shut in his face just as we drove off and left him behind. His friends who were Christians would go into heaven but he would be left standing outside because he had not repented of his sins and accepted Jesus as his Savior. He began thinking seriously and it was not long until he asked for prayer and accepted Jesus as his Savior. He had made up his mind that he was going to follow Christ and meet Him in heaven someday. Just as he thought, he has suffered persecution. His father tried to hinder him from coming to church, and threatened to beat him. One Sunday when he came to church his father was waiting for him when he got home. He got his beating but Mindali was determined to follow the Lord. After a time his father saw that he could not *hinder him with threats and beatings, so Mindali comes to church to worship his Savior unhindered. The other evening I went to town and saw a group of young men sitting together on the ground. Mindali was in the midst of them telling them about Jesus and the way of salvation.*

TRADITIONAL KAMBERI RELIGION

Most tribesmen have a religion in which they are trying to find peace with God. In learning more about various religions we often thought of Paul's statement about the Jewish people: "Brethren, my heart's desire and prayer to God for Israel is, that they might be saved. For I bear them record that they have a zeal of God, but not according to knowledge. For they being ignorant of God's righteousness, and going about to establish their own righteousness, have not submitted themselves unto the righteousness of God" (Romans 10:1-3).

One could say the same thing about the Kamberi people. They seek after God in their own way but not in God's way. They have a religion which they say is God's way for the Kamberi people to get to heaven. They revere what they call a dragon who has much to do with the running of the town. They are faithful in this man-made religion even though they remain in their darkness and find no peace with God. Most of the men belong to the Magiro fetish. The rest of the nationals belong to another Religious Society called the Agunu.

Magiro is a male-dominated religion. The women's only part is to obey the orders given, that is to make the designated number of pots of beer or other kinds of food as ordered. They are to kill their chicken at the appropriate time. When the dragon is said to come out of his hut, the women run and hide so he will not see them or they will not see him.

One day we were standing at the back door of our house when we heard the sound of the Magiro coming out of his hut. At the same time we saw two women coming along the path beside our compound, carrying large and heavy loads of wood on their shoulders. What would these women do? How would they get back to town without being seen? The two women threw their loads of wood, with their axes, calabashes, and water bottles to the ground. Then they fell to their hands and knees and began to crawl into town. They hid behind clumps of grass, a bush or a hut if one was near. The last we saw of them they were still on their hands and knees trying to get home without being seen. Fear? Yes. Darkness? Yes. But the blood of Jesus would cleanse their hearts and set them free if they would only allow Him to.

Another day it was time for every man, woman and child to kill a chicken in a neighboring town. One afternoon an elderly woman, stooped and bent and walking with a cane, came to our door. We saluted her and she said, "Za ku sayar mini da kaza?" (Will you sell me a chicken?) We asked her why she wanted a chicken. We usually bought chickens from the townspeople No one had ever asked us to sell them a chicken. As we expected, she said that it was time to kill their chickens and she was unable to buy a chicken in her town. She had come to Salka but everyone wanted to keep their chickens for their own sacrifices. In desperation, she had come to us. We sat down on the back porch with her and told her how Jesus had made the sacrifice for her, giving His life so that she could be forgiven of her sins and set free from the fear of death and have everlasting life. She listened intently but left saying, "That way may be good for you but it isn't good for me. I must have a chicken." Later we heard that she bought a chicken from a Hausa man for three times the regular price. She returned home happy that she had a chicken to offer. We never knew if she came to know Jesus before she died but most likely not.

Boys were initiated into the society when they were about ten or twelve years old. They were taken to the fetish hut where it was said that the dragon lived. Of course, they expected to see the dragon but they did not. They were probably disappointed and may even have thought of going home and telling their mother that there was no dragon in the hut. The fetish leaders all knew what their thoughts would be because they had been through the same ceremony. They might say to the young boys, "We know you expected to see a dragon when you came in here. No, there is no dragon but there is a spirit which we cannot see that watches over the town. It tells us what to do and gives orders through its mouthpiece which we must obey." They give the boys instructions and threaten them so they will not go home and tell their mothers the truth.

When the dragon comes out of his hut again, the boys begin to run and hide as before, then suddenly they stop and think, "Oh, I do not have to hide now. I belong." They run out of their compounds, happy and proud to take part with the other men and boys although they may still feel a tug at their hearts telling them they have been deceived. There is no dragon. They take part and as they get older they become more deeply involved in a way which will never bring them peace and forgiveness of their sins or prepare them to meet God. Someday they will teach their sons the same way.

It was this binding and powerful religion that the young men who had turned to Christ had left. They were suffering opposition and persecution from their parents who told them that they could not go to heaven the white man's way. The young men had found a new peace in Jesus. They were not willing to turn back even though they were refused food, beaten and threatened with death. God's grace is sufficient in every need and his power is greater than that of Satan. His power brings victory because He is Victor over Satan.

THE OPENING OF AN OUTSTATION

Our first visit to Raba had occurred during our first weeks in Salka when the Chief had been in office only a short time. Judging from his actions, he did not particularly care to have the Word of God taught to his people. Art continued to go to Raba and started a school to teach the boys and young men to read and write. As time went on we could see that the people were becoming more friendly and we rejoiced when we began to realize that God's Word was not returning to Him void. The Chief became very friendly. At first he sent us gifts of bananas and yams. It was not the gifts that made us rejoice - it was because of his change of attitude. After some time the Chief began to realize his need of a Savior.

One Sunday after a message had been given about the Lord's return and how we need to prepare for that day, he said, "I see now that we need to repent if we are to go to heaven. We are coming." He meant not only himself but also his people. Time went on and he continued to seem very interested but made no effort to receive Christ as his Savior.

A few months after our furlough, he came to our compound. He said he was ready to repent. We prayed with him and there was great rejoicing that day. He rejoiced because his sins were forgiven; we rejoiced because of answered prayer, and the angels rejoiced because a new name was written in heaven.

Shortly after the Chief's conversion, a week of meetings was held in Raba. Several young men expressed their desire to follow Jesus. Then they wanted to learn to read so they could read the Bible. They came to reading classes and an application was made for a permit to build a church.

When the permit to build a church in Raba came through, *Ba Fita* (literally, no going out) was called. That meant that no one could go to their farms or out for wood or for any other reason. The people from the town worked to build the church. The men dug the dirt, the women and girls carried the water, then the men stomped the mud. When the mud was ready to use, the women and children carried it to the building site and the men built the walls. They built half the height the first day and let it sit overnight. The next day they built the rest. As they were nearing completion on the second day, the sky was beginning to get dark and it

looked as if a big storm was coming. If they got a heavy
rain it would wash away the soft mud and the completed
work would be spoiled. When Art went to bid the Chief
farewell for the day, the Chief said it looked as if all
their work would be ruined. Art told him that it would
not rain until the roof was on. The Chief said, "How do
you know?" Art said, "Because I am going home and
we are going to ask the Lord to withhold the rain until
the roof is on." Later some of the men expressed their
concern to the Chief that if it rained, all their work
would be spoiled. The Chief told them that it was not
going to rain until the roof was on. They said, "How do
you know?" and the Chief said, "Because the white
man is going home to pray that God will withhold the
rain until the roof is on, and I believe it." God did
answer those prayers and it did not rain until the roof
was on. On May 11, 1951, over one hundred people
crowded into the little church as the Field
Superintendent gave the dedicatory message.

Some time after the church was opened, the Chief
asked Art what he did when he was not in Raba teaching
the boys and young men to read. Art told him that he
went to other villages too. The Chief said, "The
Kamberi people are really yours." Then he gave Art a
new name, *Magajin Kambarawa*, meaning *The
Inheritor of the Kamberi people.*

Did this fulfill the promise of Psalm 2:8? It says,
"Ask of me, and I shall give thee the heathen for thine
inheritance, and the uttermost parts of the earth for thy
possession."

Since that time the work in Raba has continued to
grow. Young men have learned to read and some of

them have attended Bible School and pastored churches. The first District Superintendent of the Kontagora District was a convert from the town of Raba. In 1987 they built their third church because the first and second were too small.

KURA

Kura is a village about six miles south of Salka. The Gospel had been taken to this village for some time before we arrived in the country. When there were no missionaries in Salka, DanDodo rode his bicycle there frequently to hold a service and tell the people about the way of salvation through Jesus. When the Bible School opened in Salka, some of the students would go nearly every Sunday to hold a service.

When Miss Hollenbeck was stationed in Salka with us, after becoming acquainted with the work, she made arrangements to spend a week in Kura. After returning she wrote: *There were three services the first Sunday. The attendance was good and for diversion we played some Hausa records on the gramophone. They enjoyed this. Each day some time was given to playing these records. There are Gospel messages and singing on them.*

Early Sunday morning I found that some of the followers of the fetish called 'Agunu' were preparing for something. They met in front of the fetish huts which are only a stone's throw from the church. Their work was to hunt out and destroy an evil spirit called a 'fatalawa.' This bad spirit was causing death and six children had died in the Chief's compound alone. Measles have been on an epidemic scale this year with many bad after-effects. To the fetish worshippers it was a challenge and they must do something about it. There was much drumming and dancing. They must get into the spirit of the task. Their weapon was a club which was a broken pestle such as is used in pounding grain and yam. Two days and one night were spent at the task. I saw the final act as they carried away a strange looking bundle which appeared to be mostly grass, but the evil spirit was inside and women and children watched and hoped, I suppose, that one more enemy was gotten rid of. My heart was burdened for them, and I had an opportunity to tell them of the One who can cast out devils, the One who conquered Satan for Himself and all of us.

Another time she and Miss Eileen Lageer spent another week in Kura preaching and visiting the people. At this time one young married man, Sharamu, stepped out for the Lord. He was the young people's leader in the Magiro fetish. He took a good stand for the Lord for a few months. He resigned the position he had in the fetish and strong opposition arose. He became afraid to eat the food or drink the water his wives fixed for him because they or someone else might have poisoned it. Sharamu became very ill and one day someone came in to Salka and said to Art, "Mai gida, (as they called Art most of the time), Sharamu is very sick. If you want to see him alive you better come quickly." Art got in the pick-up and went to see him right away. He was sick but Art encouraged him, read a portion of Scripture to him and had prayer committing him to the Lord for His care over him. Sharamu was encouraged and continued to walk with the Lord as he got better. Sometime later he came home from his farm in the evening. He was tired and still had to get himself something to eat. As soon as he had completed his meal, he went to bed. When he woke up in the morning, he saw something hanging over his doorway. Immediately he knew what it was. It was one of the most powerful charms that their people could get! They had hung it over his doorway. It was supposed to be so powerful that if anyone even walked under it he would die. He knew they were after his life. With that, he gave up following the Lord Jesus who had more power than any charm or even the evil one himself.

After this, students from the Bible School continued to go to Kura, but there was little or no response to the Gospel for a long time. In fact, it was about eighteen years later when another married man decided he would follow the Lord. He faced opposition too because the townspeople did not want a Christian in the town. Alaji was rather a quiet man and went on his way still walking with the Lord. He could read the Bible and found strength from the Lord to help him in every time of need. After some months those who were opposing him so strongly seemed to get tired of doing so. Apparently they were not making much impression on Alaji and they began to ignore him until most of the opposition ceased.

A short while later some young men stepped forward and said that they had been watching Alaji and decided that if he gave up, they would know that there was nothing to this Christianity they were hearing about. But if he stood and faced the opposition they, too, wanted to become Christians. Of course, neither Alaji nor anyone else knew of their decision. One day several of them stepped out for the Lord. It was not long until others followed. Soon there was quite a group of Christians and they wanted to build a church in which they could meet to worship the Lord.

Satan was not yet willing to give up, and opposition continued in various ways but the church grew. Application had been made to the Chief for a plot of ground where they wanted to build the new church. The Chief seemed reluctant to grant them permission for a church and kept putting them off. At this time we had made arrangements to go out to Kura and spend several days with the people. We knew that permission had not yet been granted for the plot of ground the Christians wanted, but we did not know any particulars about it.

After getting our camper settled in Kura, we went to town to greet the Chief. After the usual salutations, the Chief said, "Did you hear about the letter I got from Sokoto?" (Sokoto was the State capital at the time. Anything that came from Sokoto was really official and they had to pay attention to it.) We said, "No, we have heard nothing about a letter." The Chief sent a man to get the letter and gave it to us to read. It said that he was to have every place of worship in the town torn down if it was not a mosque, and if permission was sought to build a place of worship, it must not be granted. That would include the Magiro fetish hut which disturbed the Chief very much. Also he was not to grant the Christians permission for a plot of land to build a church. It stated further that if he did not listen to what was written in the letter they would come and take care of him. The Christians knew of the letter but had not told us.

We questioned the Chief about how he got the letter. It did not have a stamp or a postmark on it, so it had not come through the mail. The Chief said that when he walked into his entrance hut one morning it was on the floor. Someone had apparently slipped it under his door. Art told him that the Federal Government had granted permission for the mission to have a church in Kura a long time ago, and the papers were still on file at Mission Headquarters. "Who would've had authority over the Federal Government to prevent permission previously granted?" he asked the Chief. The Chief began to feel a little more at ease about the situation and the Christians were encouraged and continued to pray for permission for a plot of ground. Eventually a plot of ground to build a church was granted and the church was built. A pastor was sent to lead this flock.

Later the people found out that the letter that had been slipped under the Chief's door was written by a young man who had been studying in a Moslem school in Sokoto. He was learning how to prove to people that the Bible was not enough for their salvation. He was a Kura boy but they chased him out of town because of what he had done.

Alaji passed away during our last term on the field with real victory in the Lord. He was in the hospital in Kontagora during his last illness. Some of his family and friends were with him and he was admonishing them to wholly follow the Lord. He was singing hymns and all the people, even the nurses, marvelled that one so sick and with so little hope, could so rejoice. He passed away praising God and his last words were, "I have made it" as he slipped on to be with his Savior.

BEGINNING A BIBLE SCHOOL

A decision at the Annual Field Conference in October, 1950, set the direction for our work and our future ministry. Before the Conference met, there was talk of a need for a Bible Training School in the Hausa speaking area to train pastors, Sunday School teachers, Christian leaders and laymen. When Rev. Sloat, the Field Director, asked me if I would be willing to be the principal and teacher for the Bible School, my reaction was, "I can't do that. I am not a teacher and have had no teacher training." He seemed confident that I could do it, saying, "You are a natural born teacher." Someone has said that the many students who were trained under my ministry prove that I did a good job and was capable of the task that was entrusted to me. I can only thank the Lord for His help and guidance through the years or such would not have been possible. It has been said that God never asks us to do anything that we cannot do with His help. I know that it was His help that made it possible for me to accomplish what was accomplished.

Near the first of December, 1950, a group of men began digging our sweet potatoes which had been planted at the back of the compound. In a short time many little pegs were sticking up - a building program was in progress. One Saturday morning after the foundations for the houses had been dug, a stream of men, women and children was marching past our house. The men were coming to dig clay and the women, with calabashes of water on their shoulders, to help prepare the mud for building. Each of the five sections of the town agreed to build two round native-style huts which were to house the Bible School students and their families coming from the Zuru area. On Monday the first mud was poured into the foundations and by Wednesday the walls of the ten houses were finished. The supervisor had a big job keeping the door and window frames straight while one person was pushing mud from one way and someone else from the other way. The people from surrounding villages brought thatching grass and God gave strength and help. On Saturday, January 27, 1951, when we heard the motor of the hospital truck, we praised God that the students Rev. Paul Ummel was bringing from Zuru would have a place to sleep that night.

On February 4, 1951, the missionaries, eleven Bible School students, and some of the African Christians met for a time of prayer asking God for His help and blessing in the new work that we were beginning under His guidance. Our thoughts for the day were based on 2 Timothy 2:15: "Study to shew thyself approved unto God, a workman that needeth not to be ashamed, rightly dividing the word of truth."

The principal brought out the thought that if we are to go forth as workmen of God, in which there is no cause for shame, we must first give ourselves wholly to God and live lives acceptable to Him. It is only under the leadership of the Holy Spirit that we can rightly divide the Word of truth. Therefore, we must study and give ourselves completely to Him so that he can prepare us to be workmen that would please Him.

The next morning at eight o'clock the school bell

rang and the students gathered for their first class period. Some of them had never attended a regular school before. They had learned to read and write from their African pastors. Some had very little previous Bible training but they all came with great eagerness to learn the Word of God and with hearts open to receive whatever God had in store for them. This desire made teaching easy and the time spent in the classroom and study was profitable and pleasant to both the students and the two teachers, Miss Hollenbeck and myself.

We were thankful that the complete Bible was already translated into Hausa. There were very few textbooks so there was a lot of translation to do and courses to prepare.

Although the wives of the students did not attend regular classes with the men, there were classes for them which included instruction in reading.

After school had started in February, Rev. Sloat visited the different mission stations in August. In his report concerning Salka, he wrote: *The time spent in visiting the Bible School classes will long be remembered. The Spirit of God was present as the Word was being taught. The presence in the class of one young man from the backward, pagan Kamberi tribe is indeed a victory in itself. In this group of young men the foundation is being laid for a real advance in the work of the Lord. God seemed to be doing the 'exceeding abundantly' in Salka.*

BAPTISMAL SERVICE AT SALKA

The second year of the Bible School's operation, all the students returned after vacation with great anticipation and the excitement of seeing God's work grow. Students were going out to villages regularly on Sundays and God was beginning to build his church in those villages. After the dry season, when the rains began and the streams filled up, a baptismal service was planned. Art tells about this service which was held in July, 1952.

It is impossible for me to put into words the joy that was ours during the first baptismal service in Salka. However, I am writing to you about this service to remind you that missions do pay. It is now over twenty-nine years since missionaries came to Salka. There has not always been a missionary to carry on the work here but many years have been spent in sowing seed. Those who labored here previously were not privileged to see many accept Christ. In the past few years a small number have received Christ as their Savior. On July 16, there were sixteen baptized during the first baptismal service to be held in Salka. Six of these were Kamberi young men from Salka. The other young men were Dakkarkaries from Zuru area who are here in Bible School. Rev. Sloat, who labored here for almost nine years, was able to attend this service and baptized some of the candidates. Each one of the sixteen gave his or her testimony to the forgiveness of their sins before entering the water for baptism. The presence of the Lord was felt in our midst.

A few hours after the baptismal service we gathered in the church for the first communion service here. Rev. Sloat brought the message on the Lord's supper and then those who were baptized partook of their first communion. Before Rev. Sloat left, the six Kamberi

young men's names were placed on the Church roll
here as the first members. They chose their delegate to
attend the African Church Conference to be held later
that month.

BIBLE SCHOOL GRADUATES BEGIN WORK

In October, anticipating school completion in December, the African Church Conference met at Zuru and the new graduates were stationed for the coming year. Three of them were to pastor village churches in the Zuru area. In some of these places the church was strong. In others it was weak and some had fallen into the snares of Satan.

Mai Kyau was to work at the new station in Gurai with Rev. and Mrs. Virgil Pollock. Audu went to Agara'iwa where a new station was being built. These two needed to learn the language of the tribe where they were to work. Ibrahim was to work with the Boettgers at Shabanda and go on evangelistic tours during dry season. Bitrus and Hana Aiki were also going on the evangelistic tours. Even though they were not assigned a church, we expected the evangelistic efforts to produce some new converts. These two would be free to remain in such villages and start new churches. What a great work! Indazo, the only Kamberi in the class, was sent to a new outstation about twenty-seven miles from Salka where the people had been wanting a church and school for over two years. These men felt the weight of responsibility but their trust was in a great God who promised to be with us always. God never fails.

A LOPSIDED CHURCH

At one time there were two Christian Kamberi women in Salka. The leper woman who came back to the Lord during our first term was one. Asulu, Daniya's wife, was the other. The leper woman died and Daniya's family moved to Tungam Magajiya to work in the hospital. Now there were no Christian women in Salka again.

Art had often made the statement that we were building a lopsided church. No, not because we did not have a level, but we were building only with men, no women. We did try to reach the women by visiting in their compounds. From Scripture Text calendars, we took pictures and told the Bible stories to the women. We invited the women to church and to the Savior but the women would say, "Tell my husband."

Women believed that they could not learn. Their lot was to bear children and to do hard physical labor. Their part in the traditional religion was to follow the orders given to them. Women did not participate actively in their society. Their belief was that if their husbands followed the fetish faithfully, they would be included in the final reward. If the Christian way was the right way and their husbands followed it, they would be cared for in the hereafter too. Their reply, "Tell my husband," covered their responsibility. When they were invited to attend church, they would say, "Ban iya karatu ba," meaning "I can't read." They watched from a distance as the men attended church meetings. After Connie and Earl were born, once in awhile a couple women would slip into the church to see the white babies, hoping they would get to touch their light brown hair or their soft white skin. But religion, no, it was not for them.

Miss Eileen Lageer came to Salka in 1951 to study the Hausa language. She did the dispensary work which allowed Miss Hollenbeck more time for the Bible School. After Eileen was in Salka for some time, she felt a burden for the Kamberi women and wrote the following poem which was printed in the *Missionary Banner* in February, 1952.

HEART'S BURDEN

I never saw a woman pray
In all this Kamberi tribe;
I never knew a one who felt
That God was by her side.
I've never seen her shed a tear
Nor sigh about her sin;
I've never heard the faintest cry
To ask the Savior in.
I've never heard a single one
Inquire about the Way;
Nor show an anxiousness to learn
What lies beyond today.
I do not think she even knows
That she may go to heaven;
That she, too, has a soul to save
And sins to be forgiven.
But never have I seen one yet
Who does not fear to die,
But desperately clings to life
To leave it with a cry.
Someday the countless blood-washed throng
Shall all God's glory share;
O, tell me, Father - will there be
No Kamberi woman there?

The following month, March, 1952, there was another poem published in the *Banner* which was written by Eileen's sister, Mrs. Bernice Kirkwood. It was an answer to the one written by Eileen.

A BURDENED HEART

No praying women in that dark tribe,
No tear nor sigh for sin
No anxious heart inquiring why
Christ died their soul to win.
Did we not send that loved one dear
To tell the heathen blind
That thro' the blood-bought Son of God
Eternal life should find?
Does she not teach that Kamberi
The Gospel's truth and light;
Does she not point the way to heaven
Redeemed from sin's dark night?
But wait, I know she gave her all,
Left loved ones and many dear kin
Could it not be I am the cause
The Kamberi still live in sin?
Have I prayed enough and wept the tears,
That she has failed to see
No Kamberi woman in heaven's realms
Oh, Lord, let this not be!
My prayer, O Lord, I pray to thee
That these hearts burdened down with sin
May soon, O God, with joy behold
And shine with Thy love from within.
My tears, O Lord, o'erflow my eyes,
These tears that now can fall,
I pray Thee melt those hearts of stone
And turn to Thee, Lord of All.

Some years later when we were home on furlough, the Junior Missionary Society had a contest. The children were to write a missionary poem or a missionary story. Our son, Earl, who was beginning to share the burden of our work, entered the contest. He wrote both a poem and a story and won first prize on both but was given only one prize. After some women in Salka had turned to the Lord, he took Eileen's poem and wrote a response.

COURAGE TO PRAY

I never saw a woman pray
In all this Kamberi tribe
I never knew a one who felt
That God was by her side.
Until one bright and shining day
While fetish drums were beating
The dragon marching through the town
And women their beer were making.
Already the men were feasting
When a little woman came
To inquire about the Jesus' Way
And ask forgiveness in His name.
I heard that little woman pray
For God her sins to wash away.
It took great courage that prayer to pray
While the fetish dragon marched on his way.
But with the help of God
She told her tribe the way,
And in answer to our prayer
She taught them how to pray.
Sixteen the number was that came
To attend the women's meetings
To seek guidance of the Lord
And strength to overcome the demons.
Until the gathering of the saints
Lord, may our prayers not cease
That the whole Kamberi tribe
Be loosed from Satan's leash.

WHERE CAN WE FIND WIVES?

During our second term some of the Christian young men came to our compound and told Art they had some questions. Art asked what they were.

They said, "We have been reading in the Bible where it says, 'Be ye not unequally yoked together with unbelievers' (2 Corinthians 6:14). Does that mean that we Christians should not take non-Christians to be our wives? Where will we get wives since there are no Kamberi Christian girls?"

What could we say? Could we tell them that God knows there are no Christian Kamberi girls so He would understand if they took pagan wives? No, we could not tell them that.

We said, "Let's pray and ask God to work in the lives of some of the girls so they will become Christians."

Their next question was, "When will there be Christian Kamberi families who can read the Bible and pray together like you do with your family?"

Again all we could say was, "Let's pray about it." We knelt in prayer and asked God to work in some way so there would be Christian girls and women in the Kamberi tribe, and that there would soon be Christian Kamberi families to have family devotions.

When it was nearly time for us to come home again, two of the married young men came to our compound and said they wanted to know what to do. They felt that God was calling them to Bible School. There was a rule that if a married man came to school, he and his wife must live in the houses provided for the students. Their wives were not Christians and they might not agree to come and live on the Bible School compound. If their wives would not agree, what should they do? Those making the rules for the school felt that it was important for the wives to be Christians also if the men were going to be pastors or other full-time Christian workers when they finished school. Also, even if the wives were Christians, most of them could not read. They needed some training to make good pastors' wives. The problem was taken to the Lord right then. We also promised to ask people in America to pray that these wives would agree to go with their husbands.

God answered prayer. When school opened about two months later, these two women, both named Ladi, had moved out to the Bible School with their husbands. Yes, God was faithful.

Both wives attended the Bible Classes and reading classes along with the women from other tribes who were in school. They attended chapel and heard the Gospel preached. They lived on the compound and began to notice a difference between the Christian families and other families. They saw the Christian men treat their wives and children with love and care. After some months they accepted Christ.

When Magiro came out again, both of them were still afraid and wanted to hide but their husbands told them that was not necessary now that they had become Christians. It was hard for them to escape from the fear they had been taught. One day their husbands took them out to the bush away from town and people and showed them how the noise of the dragon was made by men. They assured them that there was no dragon to fear. By God's help they were able to release their fear and be set free from it through Christ.

After these two women began attending church, other women began to get interested. Why couldn't they go too? A few would get brave and come to church. Then some of them accepted the Lord as their Savior.

After we were away from Salka for a while, I went back to attend a women's meeting. There were sixteen women present. The Kamberi women led the services and sang but they had a pastor as their speaker. How different from what it had been a few years before! We could say, "What God has done is marvelous in our eyes." The women's work has continued to grow through the years and the church is no longer a lopsided chuch. As many women as men attend the services now. There are Christian homes with family altars. In answer to prayer, there are Christian girls for the young men to marry.

TREKKING

Trekking is defined as a trip involving difficulties or complex organization; to make one's way arduously. Art has done a lot of trekking during our years in Nigeria - by foot, by bicycle, by motorcycle, by pick-up and, a few times, by canoe. He has slept in entrance huts with the goats and sheep roaming through, in shelters made of grass mats, in a tent, in the back of the pick-up and in later years, he used a 1960 Del-Ray camper on the back of the pick-up. Many times Art, along with carriers bearing his loads on their heads, left for the villages early in the morning before the sun was too hot.

As the day progressed the heat of the sun became more intense. They might stop for a few minutes of rest in the shade of a tree along the way but then would trudge on until they arrived in the village where they planned to stay overnight or for a couple of days. They would arrive in the late afternoon, tired, hungry, thirsty and dirty but, to make good use of the time, they would have a service at eight or nine o'clock at night whenever the people gathered. A record player attracted the people as it gave out the message of salvation and God's love and forgiveness in their own language. One time in a Fulani (nomadic people who traveled with their cattle) encampment, some of the women walked around the gramophone, looking it over very well. Finally they asked Art to open the box and let the boy out so they could see him.

In the beginning years in Nigeria, Art did most of his trekking within a twelve-mile radius of Salka. He felt it was important to reach villages frequently instead of traveling long distances where he could not get back again for several months or even a year or two. Also, if someone asked Jesus to come into his heart, Art felt that the person must be discipled - taught to read the Word and pray and learn to walk according to God's Word. A new Christian is like a newborn baby. It needs to be fed to grow. No one would put a bottle beside a new baby and say, "Here drink this when you get hungry," and then leave the baby there alone for a year. Neither should a new Christian be left with a Bible and instructions to read it when he gets into difficulty or needs encouragement. New Christians need to be taught, so Art concentrated on those villages closer to

Salka in the first terms of his missionary career.

When the Bible School was opened and students were given practical work assignments, Art would go with them to the villages on Sundays. Sometimes he would take three or four of them and they would go to a village for the weekend. On these visits they would visit in the compounds during the day, meeting the people and becoming acquainted with them, and talking to them in small groups or individually as they found them. In the evening after the people returned from their farms and had their evening meal, they would hold a service. Most of the people in town would attend these services. This ministry has paid off and today there are churches in a number of these villages. Although there still may not be a church building in all of them, there are small groups of Christians in most of them. This is the true church. The Bible School students are student pastors in several of them and continue to go to these villages regularly.

FURLOUGH TIME AGAIN

Bible School graduation was over and it was time for us to go home for furlough. Immediately after school was out, we began packing our things into boxes to be stored. Missionaries quickly become experts at packing and unpacking. We were getting the house ready for Rev. and Mrs. Paul Ummel who were taking our place in Salka.

One day when Art drove into town to take care of business, the pick-up caught on fire. We did not know why but some damage was done. The covering on the wires was burned, the carburetor bowl was broken and the flexible gas line was beyond repair. Art could not go to the garage and buy new parts or even to the junkyard to find used ones anywhere around Salka. It took a lot of ingenuity to get it going but, praise to the Lord, He guided and soon it was running again. Going down country it seemed to be running on four cylinders instead of six but we had a safe trip to Jebba. The next day Art and Russell Sloat worked on it. They changed some of the spark plug wires around and it worked fine again.

On December 9, the John Bontrager family and our family were booked to sail on the S.S. Aureol. That morning John and Betty, Art and I, and some other missionaries who were also sailing took our suitcases and some of our baggage down to the docks. The children stayed at the S.I.M. Mission house until Art and John went back to get the rest of the baggage and the children. Betty and I stayed with our things in the customs shed. Art and John were planning to come right back so we could get our things through customs and onto the ship before it set sail. However they did not come. and they *did* not come. Time was getting shorter and shorter and Betty and I were getting rather anxious. Finally, I saw Art coming through the crowd hanging onto the children's hands. Connie was crying. Mr. Harrison from the S.I.M. Mission had been bringing them back when they had a minor accident. No one was badly hurt but they were shook up a bit and the car was damaged. The police had come and, since the car was a left-hand drive instead of a right-hand one, they thought Art was the driver of the car and would not let him go. It took some time to persuade them that Art was not the driver, but when they agreed, Art, John, and the children got taxis and came on to the docks. They got there in time to load our things on the ship. Again we praised God for His protection for them. The accident could have been much worse, and someone could have been seriously injured, but God was watching over them.

The trip on the ocean was rather rough and cold, but we arrived safely in St. Johns, New Brunswick. We had spent Christmas on the ship and were on the train crossing from Sarnia, Ontario, to Port Huron, Michigan, when the guns went off and the bells were ringing the old year out and the new year in.

On January 21, Art started deputation work to share with the people what God was doing in Nigeria. The number of converts was increasing and God was working. His desire was to challenge people to continue to pray for the Kamberi people that many more might come to the Lord and know Him as their personal Savior.

PART III

TRAVELING AGAIN

Another furlough behind us, we said our farewells to family and friends as we prepared to return to Nigeria for our third term. This time we did not say goodbye to Art's Mother. She had gone to be with her Lord during our second term so she was not home when we arrived for furlough. My Mother and sister took us to Toronto, Canada, where we took the train to Montreal and met Mrs. Edma Brubacher and Miss Annie Yeo. We sailed to England on the Empress of Australia and then boarded another ship to Lagos, Nigeria.

We arrived in Salka six days before Christmas. Things were in a turmoil as Paul and Phoebe Ummel were moving out of the house we were moving into. Edma Brubacher was moving into the other house as she had been stationed in Salka to help in the Bible School. The Ummels went to Shabanda to celebrate Christmas. We had a good Christmas in Salka with Edma. It was good to be home again. The welcome by the Nigerians really made us feel wanted and appreciated. It did not take many days before we were back into the routine of the work. It soon seemed that we had not really been away.

SCHOOL TIME

Connie had started school in America during our furlough. She attended part of first grade in the spring when we got home and a few more weeks in the fall just before we left. Now it was time for her to really get settled into school at Hillcrest in Jos.

Hillcrest was a school started for missionaries' children by the Church of the Brethren Mission. It is located in Jos where it is cooler than most areas of Nigeria. Jos is situated on the plateau where the elevation is higher than that of most of the mission stations.

When the United Missionary Society missionaries' children became of school age, the U.M.S. leased a property for a home for the school children. This was called Rock Haven because of the many rocks. Rock Haven was about four miles from Hillcrest School. The children were transported to school in a van.

On January 18, 1954, we took Connie to Mokwa to travel to Jos with the Traubs who were taking their boys to school. On the way home, it seemed that no one had anything to say. Even Earl hardly said a word until we were nearly to Kontagora, about ninety miles on our way. We knew that God would watch over Connie and care for her in answer to our prayers, but we missed her very much.

Seven months later, when the new term began, it was time for Earl to go to school too. It was hard on us to let the first child go, but it was still harder to see them both go. We felt like grandparents with all their children grown up and away from home, but our children were only six and eight years of age.

There were many things we did not have such as

electricity, running water, telephone, a fan to cool us - just a mud house with a thatched roof and cement floor - but we never counted the absence of these things a sacrifice. Probably the only, or at least the greatest, sacrifice we made was to be separated from our children for four and a half months at a time. We did thank the Lord that there was a school in Nigeria where they could go because missionaries before us had to leave their school-age children in the States for three or four years at a time.

The children were taught to write letters to their parents every week, beginning the very first week in first grade. At first the teacher wrote the letters on paper and the children traced over the lines she had made. Later, they copied from the board what the teacher had written until the children began to write short sentences by themselves. Those letters were all precious even though the parents all got similar letters that did not carry much news of their child and took ten days to two weeks to reach them. The houseparents wrote to the parents occasionally which helped. Of course, there were many things we would have liked to hear about our children and many questions we had which were never answered. God cared for them and we were thankful for the weeks of vacation that came after each semester.

BIBLE SCHOOL OPENS AGAIN

The week after Connie left for school, the Bible School began another term. Although Mrs. Brubacher was the principal that year, the staff had many responsibilities outside school hours as well as teaching in the classes. The students and their families lived on the school compound. When there was sickness or a baby to be delivered, the students came to the missionaries for help - whether day or night. Once in a while there were emergencies and someone needed to be taken to the hospital which was a trip of one hundred miles each way. As in any school, the teachers have to prepare their lessons and materials and correct papers. Since there were few textbooks in Hausa, the teachers had to prepare the courses as well as teach them. This required some translation work. One could not just take a textbook from America and translate it into Hausa. It had to be adapted to the culture and customs of the people who were being taught. Many illustrations in an American book could not be used, for the people there would not understand the meaning.

For example, one Sunday morning a missionary who was preaching used the illustration of a bridge which opens up to let ships pass through and then closes again. The illustration was not appropriate because these people make bridges by cutting down trees from the bush and placing them over a stream, then putting grass on top of them so that the dirt which they placed on top of the grass would not fall through. How could they understand the kind of bridge she was talking about? To make it even more complicated, instead of using the word for bridge, she was using the word for a broken pot. Later when some of the mission compound staff were asked if they understood the illustration, they said, "Ba sosai ba, (Not really) but you folks in America do so many wonderful things that we thought maybe a broken pot could open up so a ship could go through."

I prepared many courses that were taught in the Bible School and later revised or rewrote some of them as the occasion demanded. The school started with a two-year course. Then a third and a fourth year were added. As the educational standard rose in Nigeria, a two-year English course was started. Finally the Hausa course was decreased to three years and the English course increased to three years. Eventually the school in Salka was divided. The Hausa school remained in Salka and a new English school was opened in Tungam Magajiya.

During our first school term back, a series of meetings were held with Rev. and Mrs. Grant Sloss as speakers. Rev. Sloss spoke to the students in chapel every morning and spoke in the church for the evening service. Mrs. Sloss spoke to the women every day. Two of the Bible School women accepted the Lord as their Savior that week and a number of spiritual victories were won. The students had a prayer meeting every day and their wives had another one. We missionaries had a time of prayer every day and God answered prayer.

After the services, we took the Slosses back to Share where they were living and then went on to Ilorin. Art had some committee meetings to attend there. On June 3, we went out to the Ilorin Airport and met Connie and the rest of the children as they came home from school for a month's vacation. What a glad reunion for both children and parents.

One evening after having tucked the children in bed under their mosquito nets, Edma, Art and I were sitting on the front porch of our house when our conversation was suddenly interrupted by a shrill scream from Connie. She had gotten up to go to the bathroom. Art dashed into the house, through the living room, into the bedroom and there he met a cobra coming into the bedroom from the bathroom. A cobra in the few feet between him and his daughter! A cobra in the few feet between him and his gun! For some reason, which was definitely God's protection, Connie stayed still instead of trying to run to her Daddy. Soon the snake crawled out of the house onto the porch where he met his fate.

The spitting cobra is able to spit his venom for nine to twelve feet and is very accurate in his aim which is often for the eyes or nose. If this venom hits one in the eye, the teardrops become thick like gelatin and the eye becomes red and is very painful. It may cause temporary blindness if not treated immediately. Therefore cobras are not desirable companions to have either in the house or around the compound.

DANDODO'S WIFE PASSES ON

July 1 was a bad day for us. Dandodo had come to work that morning before his wife and children were up. About the middle of the forenoon someone came and told him that his wife was sick and he should come home. He went home and soon came back to get some medicine. She had dysentery. I got some medicine from the dispensary and took it into town to her, but I could hardly believe my eyes when I saw her. Her eyes were sunken in and she was very dehydrated and weak. She took the medicine hoping to begin feeling better in a short time. I went home praying for her but about two o'clock word came that she had passed away. What a shock to everyone! We do not know if she was prepared to meet God at the last moment or not. She seemed anxious for us to pray with her when we saw her at noon, but we have no assurance that she was ready to go. She knew the way. DanDodo had been a Christian for a long time. Many had witnessed to her and tried to get her to come to church but she continued in her own way. Perhaps she realized that the end was near and did call upon the Lord to be saved. We do not know.

DanDodo's wife had a baby boy about a year old as well as four other children. The daughter went to live with her maternal grandmother who was not a Christian. DanDodo brought the baby to us as it is difficult to feed young children when the mother dies for they have no milk available for them. I could hardly collect my thoughts that afternoon to get Connie and Earl's suitcases packed and ready for them to leave for school the next day. The day after they left for school, Dan-Dodo, Art and I took the baby to an orphanage of the Sudan Interior Mission in Wushishi - about one hundred thirty miles from Salka. DanDodo could not care for the baby and, since I was teaching school, I was not able to take care of the baby either. DanDodo wanted to take him to the orphanage where he would be brought up in a Christian environment and would hear the Word of God and come to know Christ as his Savior. The sad end of the story is that, although the nurses and workers at the orphanage did all they could with the materials and equipment they had, the baby absolutely refused to eat either by bottle, cup or spoon and he, too, died a short time later. God took one more of His precious jewels.

THE SECOND HAUSA CAMP MEETING

The first Hausa Camp Meeting was held in 1953 while we were home on furlough. The second one was held in March, 1954, about three months after we returned from furlough. Art was there to attend and he gave us a report: *The second Hausa camp meeting was held at Bedi in March. Christians from almost every mission station and outstation of the U.M.S. in northern Nigeria came. On Saturday night there were about sixty present. Before the 6:30 prayer meeting Sunday morning, many more had arrived. Some of them had walked since two or three o'clock in the morning. The attendance was twice that of last year. Early morning prayer meeting attendance was almost one hundred percent. Only those who were sick did not come. After a short message on prayer, the group divided and gathered in small groups for prayer.*

It was a real encouragement to see the response during altar services. Many confessed to not tithing and sought forgiveness. God had spoken to some about working on Sunday and they asked God to forgive them. God spoke to some about beating up their wives in anger, and they made things right with God. One man sent for his wife and made things right with her at the altar. Adultery and fornication seem to be the besetting sins in Africa. Some confessed they had been tempted and had fallen but they found forgiveness in Jesus. Praise His name!

The one question uppermost in the minds of the Christians was, "Why were camp meetings not started long ago?" They are receiving much value from these gatherings and plan to return and bring others with them.

FATHER AND SON FIND THE LORD

As the work in Nigeria continued to grow and the Nationals were trained, they helped to reach out into other villages and spread the Gospel story. Pastor Kibo and Pastor Indazo held meetings in the village of Wando about twelve miles from Salka. Indazo told of their trip: *Mallam Kibo and I went to Wando to tell the people of Him who has prepared the way of escape. We told them neither the prophet, Mohammed, nor the Magiro, nor the Agunu, nor the blood of rams or of chickens are sufficient for redemption. Nothing is sufficient except the blood of Jesus who died in our place. They listened very well. They were Kamberi people who followed the fetishes.*

We preached day after day and spent much time in the bush praying, asking God to show us what to do. We visited from house to house getting acquainted with many people. One day I had to return to Salka for a few hours. When I got back, Mallam Kibo told me that seven people had come to him asking the way of repentance. Kibo talked with them and then told them to wait there until I got back. They said they did not want me to know. I am a Kamberi and they were afraid that I would tell other Kamberi. Fear overwhelmed them and they left. Don't say that God is not able! He does wonderful things in answer to prayer. Two of these men came back and asked for prayer. They repented of their sins and did not care who knew it. One was the Chief of the fetish of the town, and the second was his oldest son. We prayed with them. They confessed their sins and be-

came children of God.

AN EVANGELISTIC TOUR

Art and I and two Nigerians had visited an area where one could drive along the motor road and not see a church for one hundred twelve miles. We visited in a strong Moslem town where many of the people had never seen a white person and certainly not a white woman. The women were in purdah, under strict regulation, and were not allowed out of their compounds except at certain times. Men could not enter these Moslem compounds to visit but women could. I visited in the women's compounds. Since they had never seen a white woman, they wanted to touch my skin and hair to be sure I was a woman like them. When we returned from that trip, a burden for these people was on Art's heart and he wanted to return. He asked Mallam Kibo, an evangelist, to accompany him. Art writes about it:

After seeking God's direction and blessing upon this trip, we are off for Maga, about twenty-seven miles from Zuru. Recently an evangelistic team had found good interest in this town. Shortly after our arrival, a young man came to us inquiring about the way of salvation. We talked with him. After the evening service, he repented and asked Jesus into his life. That night we went to sleep praising God for this first convert in the town.

Saturday morning it seemed that Satan was trying to hinder the work as I was not feeling well physically. However, God had work for us in Maga and that afternoon another soul sought forgiveness through the precious blood of Jesus. We had a good visit with the Chief who is friendly and interested in the Gospel Story. He made two requests of us. The first was that we start a school in his town to teach them the true way; and the second was that we help him get a Hausa Bible so he can read God's Word for himself. The door to his town is open and we want to keep in touch with these new Christians until a pastor can be sent there.

Our plans were interrupted Sunday when a Fulani man was brought to us. He had fallen out of a tree and was badly hurt. We took him to the hospital at Tungam Magajiya. On Tuesday we left from there to go to Ribah to join Mallam Bawa.

On the way to Ribah we heard about two young men who had recently repented in Kainya in spite of the fact that the Chief of Kainya had not allowed any preaching of the Gospel in his town for years. Mallam Bawa had already gone to Kainya so we decided to go there too. It was a real privilege to preach to a group of people who listened as attentively as they did. We felt led to spend Wednesday there also, and that afternoon we were able to lead another young man to the Lord. After the evening service a message came saying that the old Chief, father of the present Chief, wanted to see us. In the dark entrance of the Chief's compound we found an old blind man. He was blind physically but seeking for sight spiritually. After the salutations were completed, his words were, "I want to repent." He told us that he was the one who had hindered the preaching of the Gospel in Kainya. After we prayed, he cried out to God to receive him as His child. From then on he had a burning testimony for the Lord. When he passed away, he was buried by the Christians from Ribah.

Thursday morning we left Kainya for Wasagu and Bena. Between these towns there are a number of villages where we stopped to sow the seed of God's Word. We preached to many who had never heard the way of salvation before. We wonder how much of the truth they were able to grasp from hearing the story only once. After leaving Bena on Saturday morning we preached in a number of villages along the way until we came to Kakiffum where we spent the night. In Kakiffum we had an opportunity to speak to the children of the government school as well as to a number of adults who gathered to hear the message we brought to them. Sunday we rode our bikes over to Kumbashi but were back in Kakiffum for another service Sunday evening.

Tomorrow morning we plan to start home, but tonight we are reminded of God's promise that His Word shall not return unto Him void. We trust that we have been faithful in sowing the seed and following His leading on this trip. We have been conscious of His presence all along the way. God has blessed the preaching of His Word but how long will it be before someone is able to go to these people again?

PART IV

A CHANGE - ROCK HAVEN

Before the 1955 Annual Conference, I talked to the Field Superintendent and told him that I felt a man should be the principal of the Bible School. The reason for this was discipline problems and because of the fact that in the African culture it is easier for a man to have a word of authority than it is for a woman. The students respected me and, to my knowledge, no student ever complained about a woman being principal or being head of the school. However it was my feeling that a man should be in that position.

At Conference, Rev. and Mrs. Harold Hallman were sent to Salka to take over the work of the Bible School. Art and I were stationed in Jos at Rock Haven to be houseparents to the school children when Rev. and Mrs. Earl Honsberger went on furlough in June, 1956.

Art and I packed up our things, storing most of them in Salka, as in Jos we would have only a bedroom. Kitchen, living room and dining room were all shared with the children. We moved to Jos before school was out to have some time with the Honsbergers before they left for furlough. During the time the children were on vacation we painted some of the rooms, bought wood and had it cut up ready for the cookstove for the next term, and other menial tasks to get ready for the children's return.

Fourteen children plus our two completed the family that term until Eva Mae arrived in September to add another member to the household. There was quite a bit of sickness as the measles and mumps made their way around among the children. There were also a few complications and I was glad for a doctor and nurses nearby at the S.I.M. Hospital to help with the care of the children.

At the Annual Conference in October that year, it was decided that a dorm for the children should be built, including quarters for the houseparents. Art was not a builder. Rev. and Mrs. Paul Ummel would be returning from furlough around Christmas time and they were asked to be the houseparents. Rev. Ummel would go ahead with the building project. We went to Yelwa for a few months until our furlough was due in June, 1957.

First we took two weeks' vacation in Miango at the S.I.M. Rest Home before moving to Yelwa. It was harmattan season when the dust from the Sahara desert blows across the country and shields the sun, so it was really quite cold during the time we were there. When we moved to Yelwa, it was already very warm. We were not in Yelwa a week when Eva Mae became ill. It seemed that she just could not adjust to the warmer climate. We took her to Tungam Magajiya to the doctor. It was a little cooler up there and she seemed to get better. We would go back to Yelwa and she would be worse again. Chicken pox was going around in Yelwa and, finally, the doctor said that we had better take her to America. She would have no strength or resistance to fight the disease if she got it. We got ready to leave for furlough in April instead of June as we'd planned. An S.I.M. airplane came to Yelwa and flew us to Kano. Connie and Earl flew from Jos to Kano and we met there.

When we left Kano and were up in the air where it was much cooler, Eva Mae was like a little flower bud that one could see opening up slowly. By the time we arrived in Boston, Massachusetts, the next morning she was a different baby.

We kept our appointment at Cleveland Clinic where they did many tests and observed her. They said she may have had mononucleosis but it was very seldom seen in babies. She got along real well in cooler weather. Whatever the cause of her problem, she had no special or unusual difficulties adjusting to weather when we returned to Nigeria a year later. We thank God for sparing her life and making her a strong and healthy child. Her Hausa name is *Murna* which means *rejoicing*. We rejoiced when she was born and we rejoiced again when God touched her and continued to give her life.

RETURN AND KAMASHI'S DEATH

In 1958 we returned to Nigeria for our fourth term. After our arrival we learned of the death of Kamashi, the leper man. He had died in December, 1957, while we were home on furlough. Kamashi had believed in the Lord Jesus many years before and was one of the two Christians in Salka when we arrived there in 1946. At that time there was no medicine to help leprosy and his body continued to waste away until about four years before he died. The government began supplying a new medicine which works wonders for lepers today. These little pills were too late to help Kamashi much but they did retard the progress of the disease somewhat for him. Miss Hollenbeck wrote about his death: *Kamashi's hands and feet had become mere stubs. He could not walk. He spent his time in his little round mud hut with a grass mat for a door. He could build a fire, heat some water and make some of his food. Earlier his wife had left him but came back a few years ago. An older brother and his children have ministered to his needs, which were few.*

There is a bright side to the picture - Kamashi was a happy Christian. His disfigured face would light up with a heavenly glory when he witnessed to his faith in a living Christ. He looked forward eagerly to the day when he would go to be with the Lord. Everyone in Salka knew that Kamashi did not believe or follow the heathen practices. I never called on him and felt depressed, rather I would be uplifted and encouraged. He was in a sad condition physically but spiritually he was strong and unwavering in his faith.

His relatives tell us that he said he was going to heaven and that they should not make any of their heathen sacrifices for him after his death. He said that when he died they should call the missionaries who would bury him in a Christian manner. When none of the missionaries were in town when he died, they called the African pastor, and all of the staff on the mission compound went to the burial service. I shall want to see Kamashi when I reach heaven.

DIMA, ONE LIVING, YET DEAD

Art continued to do village evangelism. Sometimes there were discouraging times as well as good times. One discouraging time concerns the story of Dima. Art shares the story:

Dima was a Christian from the town of Ubege. The pastor from Zuru and I were on the way to Ubege to hold special services. The way seemed long partly because of the heat and partly because of the rocky places where it was impossible to ride our bikes. Some of the Christian men had met us about fourteen miles from their town to take our loads on their heads for us. We arrived in Ubege before they did and waited and waited, expecting them at any time. By eight o'clock I had about one swallow of water left in my water bottle but still hopefully awaited the arrival of the carriers.

Finally, about eight-thirty, they came. They had stopped several times to rest along the way because it was so hot; then as they drew near the town, Dima had been bitten by a snake! Several men took a lantern and went immediately to the place where he was bitten and killed the viper that had bitten him. I opened my loads and took out the snake-bite kit. The tourniquet was applied, the incision was made and the suction pump applied to draw out the blood and the poison. At eleven o'clock, after doing all we could and committing the life of this young man to the tender care of the Lord, we finally went to sleep. Early Sunday morning the pastor rode his bike back to Zuru and returned with the dispenser who injected snake serum to counteract the remaining poison. Through the day much prayer went up to the throne of grace on his behalf. Monday morning the dispenser returned to Zuru and Art and the pastor cared for Dima. He had some swelling in one arm and one leg. Later I felt definitely led of the Lord to annoint Dima and God met with us. I am certain that he was drawn closer to the Lord during these days. It was a blessing to hear him pray.

Dima's pagan mother was not satisfied with the progress he was making. On Wednesday afternoon she had three pagan men give him some medicine to drink and also to rub on his body. I did not know about this until the next morning. That night Dima began to complain of pains in his stomach. Thursday evening about five-thirty he was unconscious and it seemed he did not have much longer in this world.

We again sought God on his behalf and when we returned about two hours later, he recognized us. The service that evening turned into a prayer meeting for Dima. When we checked on him after the service, he seemed much better and we went to bed thanking God for His help.

The next morning Dima ate a good breakfast and had a nice visit with his brother-in-law who was leaving to return to his home about ninety miles away. The pastor and I were to leave Ubege that morning to go to Bajida so after having prayer with Dima and thanking God for His care, I went back to pack my loads.

About ten o'clock word came that Dima had just passed away. What a shock! Was I hearing right? It did not seem possible and yet it was the truth. God had taken Dima home.

There was a funeral service that afternoon and there

was weeping and wailing but I could not help but feel
that there was rejoicing in heaven for precious in the
sight of the Lord is the death of his saints. Yes, it
happened to Dima. Thank God, he was prepared to
meet God.

ELMER'S BIRTH

When we returned for our fourth term we were
stationed in Zuru, where I was in charge of the Boarding School. We had been in Zuru about fifteen months
when Elmer Lee came to be the sixth person in our
family. He was born on September 20, 1959, and was
named after his Grandfather Chapman.

As each of the other three children had been, he was
given a Hausa name since it was difficult for the Nigerians to pronounce our American names. He was called
DanLadi because he was born on Sunday. Connie was
called Talata because she was born on Tuesday. Earl
was DanTani because he was born on Monday. We
gave Eva Mae the name Murna even though she was
born on Saturday. We did not care for the name Asibi
too much, so before the Nigerians named her, we gave
her a name. Connie and Earl were away at school when
Elmer was born so he was nearly three months old
before they saw their little brother.

REIFELS MOVE TO GURAI

In January, 1960, we moved to Gurai, which is near
the Dahomey (now Benin) border, to fill in for Virgil
and Betty Pollock while they were on furlough. Bugi
had been working in the dispensary with Mrs. Pollock
and he could speak Hausa, so I kept him as my helper

and interpreter. Bugi had lost a leg due to a large ulcer. He hobbled along by the use of a stick which he held with both hands. Art had compassion on him and set out to make him a wooden leg because artificial limbs were unavailable in Nigeria at that time. He took a board and carved and whittled at it, cutting out the center, sanded it, and then lined it with a soft cloth for the stump of his leg. He used pieces of inner tube to hold it onto Bugi's stump. Bugi thought it was a miracle. Now he could walk. What a thrill for him to walk upright like other people. Later the leg Art made began to irritate the stump of his leg. For a long time he would not tell anyone because he did not want to give up that leg. A large ulcer developed and he was taken to the hospital. By this time the Nigerian Government had a policy that helped people like Bugi to get an artificial limb. Finally Bugi got a better-fitting artificial leg.

WHERE IS BAKE?

Bake was a young married woman probably less than twenty years of age. One day she went to visit her mother with the intention of staying until her second child was born. Her first one had died when only a few days old. When I was called, Bake had already given birth to a little baby girl hours before. The compound people had tried their methods and medicine to expel a retained placenta to no avail.

Having failed in their efforts, they finally sent to the Mission Dispensary for help. I gathered together a few things, took the lamp and went to town to see if there was any help I could give her. I found the wee tiny baby still lying on the dirt floor, not having had any care. I cut the cord and one of the women in the compound took the baby to bathe it. We tried to persuade them to let us take Bake to the Baptist Hospital in Shaki, about eighty miles away, but they refused. We tried to explain what would happen if she did not get the medical attention necessary. The Chief of the town was a relative and he tried to talk them into letting her go, but they still did not agree. They seemed to think if anyone went to the hospital they would surely die. When Bake began hemorrhaging they thought that was a good sign, now the placenta would surely detach and she would soon be better.

While Bake was still quite strong and was sitting up some, the pastor's wife and I, along with an interpreter, went to talk to her about the Savior. We could not let her go on into the next world without giving her another opportunity to accept Jesus. There were several other women who listened very attentively to the message we gave Bake, and they agreed that it was a good idea to prepare to meet God. Just as the people had refused the physical help we offered, they also refused the help of the Savior who was waiting at their heart's door.

The morning after the hemorrhaging had begun, Bake's spirit departed from her body. Her body is buried in Gurai but where is Bake? We knew that if her people had agreed to let us take her to the hospital, she probably would have been well and her life spared. Or if she had only accepted the Savior, she could have spent eternity in heaven with Him.

Bake had given birth to a baby girl. We were told that if they had not come to the white people the baby would have been buried alive with the mother according to their custom. Since they had called the white people, they were afraid to do that. The grandmother came to the Mission to see if we could help them with some milk for the baby. I prepared the milk and gave it to them in a bottle with a nipple. I told them, through an interpreter, how to feed the baby and wash the bottle. In two or three days the grandmother came back and said the baby would not drink the milk. They did not want to bring the baby. I did not know if they were afraid I would keep her or what, but I told them I could not help them if they would not do as I asked them. Finally they brought her and also brought the bottle back. The milk was sour and the nipple was so full of sour milk that the baby could not drink from it. The baby took the milk very well when the bottle and nipple were clean. After that I had them bring me the bottles every day, and I sterilized them and gave them fresh milk every day.

After we moved back up country, Pollocks were again in Gurai and Mrs. Pollock continued to help them care for the baby. One time when Pollocks were away for a few days and the baby was about eighteen months old, she got diarrhea and died before they got back home.

REIFELS WORK IN AGARA'IWA

Agara'iwa is now called Agwara. We moved from Gurai to Agara'iwa when Pollocks came back to Gurai. It is a different branch of the Kamberi than we worked with in Salka. Also, their dialect of the Kamberi language is different than that of Salka.

One of the experiences that all of our family remem-

bers was a man with a very bad ulcer. Art tells the story:
*We found him in a sordid, dirty hut with a terrible ulcer
eating away at his foot. Earl and I were visiting in the
town when we found the man. He sat alone in filthy
surroundings for no one could bear to be near him. I
say this with no exaggeration; you could smell the
stench of his ulcer from twenty feet away.*

*We saluted the man and, after visiting with him,
suggested that it would be a good idea to have the foot
amputated.*

*"Oh, no," he said. "Nothing like that! God is here
and if He kills me like this, all right. But I won't go
through life with one leg." We tried to reason with him
but to no avail.*

*The man had no food, no clothes, no friends. I asked
the Christians if they had visited him and if they had
ever told him the story of Jesus.*

*"Yes," they said, "We used to take the Gospel to
him and tell him about Jesus until the ulcer got to
stinking so bad that it was impossible to stand the smell
any more, so we stayed away and left him as he was."*

*In the following days we visited him and did what we
could to help him. We offered to take him to the hospital
at Tungam Magajiya. At first he refused to go but God
was working and had a purpose in it all. Finally he
agreed to go. We took him to T.M. and left him in the
care of the doctors and nurses, trusting that God would
work in the life of this Moslem man living in spiritual
darkness.*

*We went home to pray for him and asked the Chris-
tians in Agara'iwa to pray. We wrote letters home asking people to pray for him also.*

Because of the man's physical condition, it was necessary for the doctors to build up his body with food and medication in preparation for the operation. Finally they set a date for the surgery.

A short time before the operation, when Miss Esther Cressman was visiting him, he was telling her about the Moslem religion.

"Oh, the story of Christ," he said, "There's no truth in it. Such a thing as His death and resurrection, I don't believe."

She got a Bible and read to him the story of Christ's death and resurrection from the grave.

"Well, there must be some truth to it," he admitted reluctantly. She explained the way of salvation to him.

Several days later, when the pastor from T.M. was visiting with him, he asked Jesus to come into his heart. For the next two or three days the witness of the Spirit was there as he gave his testimony. Then one day he said, "I'm so glad I let Jesus Christ come into my heart."

A few days later he died suddenly so the operation was never performed. He went to heaven with his two legs. Through the conversion of this Moslem man and his positive testimony, at least two other conversions have resulted.

AN EARLY FURLOUGH

A short time after we moved to Agara'iwa, Art and I were not feeling well and did not seem to respond to the treatment the doctor was giving us. It was decided that we should go home in December when the children came home from school instead of waiting until June as we had planned. We both had check-ups at Cleveland Clinic. They did not really determine our problems other than fatigue and stress; however, it was not until March, 1963, that the doctor finally gave his okay for me to return to Nigeria.

Connie and Earl were in ninth and tenth grades in high school in Cass City, Michigan. School was out in May so we did not return to Nigeria until June. In a class letter to our former Bible College classmates, I wrote: *We never look forward to parting with loved ones and saying goodbye but this time it was even more difficult as we left Connie behind too. She is a junior in high school and is staying with my sister in South Bend, Indiana. The Lord gave us the assurance in our hearts that we were doing His will, so we are trusting Him to be with each of us as we are separated one from another. Earl is a sophomore in high school and hopes to complete his course here in Nigeria. Eva Mae also said goodbye to Mother and Daddy and went to Jos for the first time. We appreciate the houseparents who are looking after the children. They are doing a real good job. Elmer is the only one home now and he surely misses the rest of the family, especially Eva Mae.*

Yes, we had to let go of Connie when she went off to school in Jos when she was six and again when she went to live with her Aunt Lila when she was a teenager. Connie is proud of her heritage and grateful to God and her parents for the rich life with which she has been blessed. She shares that being an M.K. (Missionary's Kid) meant experiences that none of her friends in the States had; a private school, exposure to different cultures - not just the tribes that her father had contacted - but the special trips, stopping in Europe on the way home and Stateside travels. Connie remembers when Billy Graham visited Hillcrest School in Jos. She knows that not all M.K.s had such positive experiences and some viewed the separations differently. She is very active in keeping in touch with other M.K.s through reunions and support groups.

SICKNESS STRIKES AGAIN

Our fifth term was rather difficult. It was about seven months after we arrived back on the field that Art became ill. He went to the hospital in Tungam Magajiya first and then to the S.I.M. Hospital in Jos. After that he was taken to the Government Hospital in Ibadan for thirty days. There were several diagnoses suggested, such as viral pneumonia, kidney stones, muscle spasms, spasms of the urethra, and others, but no treatment he was given for any of them seemed to be successful.

The children remember their father, when he felt the pain in his side coming, lying on the floor clutching the table leg or a chair leg and gritting his teeth until it passed. It seemed that the pain was worse in the evening when he was tired, but he continued to carry on his work as he could.

In September, 1964, we were stationed in Igbetti so that I could take over the work of the principal at the Light and Life Correspondence School, and Art could continue in village evangelism and literature work as he was able. There was talk of our returning to the States for medical attention, but that did not come about for some time. Finally, after suffering this pain for twenty-seven months, it was decided that we should go back to the Cleveland Clinic for a thorough physical examination.

When he was going through one examination on his upper arteries, he could hear one doctor say to another, "Look, there is something there. The blood is being forced back. It does not go through." They could not tell what was the cause but they decided to do exploratory surgery.

We realized how God's time is always correct. He is seldom too early and never too late. If Art had come to the clinic a month earlier, the doctors probably would not have found his trouble. They had recently received some new equipment and without that equipment they could not have found his problem. In fact, a man from Japan was teaching them how to use the machine when they examined Art.

When they performed exploratory surgery, Art was in the operating room seven hours. They found a ninety percent narrowing of the celiac artery and were able to dilate the artery and improve the blood flow. After the surgery the doctor reported that they were uncertain if they had solved his problem. He never had any more pain.

After a few days the doctor told Art that while they were doing surgery they felt something in the celiac artery. Some of the doctors did not want to open the artery, but the head doctor said, "He wants to go back to Africa, and he will never get back if we don't take care of this." They went ahead and opened the artery. The doctor said that since the celiac artery was over ninety percent closed, if it had been left alone, gangrene would have set in and they would not have been able to cure it. God had spared Art's life. If he had come home and gone to the clinic immediately when he had pains, they would not have found his problem and he would have died in a short time. When the year of furlough was over, Art had fully recovered and was ready to go back to Nigeria.

PART V

RETURN TO SALKA

Art and I lived in Mishawaka, Indiana, while Art was recovering from his surgery. Earl had graduated from high school in Nigeria just before we came home on furlough, and was planning to attend Bethel College to study for the ministry. Connie had already attended one year at Bethel. Our family wanted to be together during our furlough so, instead of living in the thumb area of Michigan, we rented a house in Mishawaka where Connie and Earl could be home and still go to college. When we returned to Nigeria, Earl moved to the Bethel campus. Connie was married. She and her husband attended Emmanuel Bible College in Kitchener, Ontario.

Art and I and Eva Mae and Elmer returned to Zuru, Nigeria for a few months. When John and Retha Moran and family returned home for furlough, we returned to Salka. I was back in the Bible School and Art continued to do village evangelism.

CROSSING ON DRY GROUND

"When can you come to Zamalo for meetings?" inquired Pastor Shirika.

"Is there a dry season road that I can travel with the pick-up and camper or will I trek in?" Art asked.

"No, there is no road now," Shirika hesitantly replied, "but we will make one."

The construction company for the Kainji Dam project had built a road which went within four miles of Zamalo. The Christians worked to make a passable road for those four miles. A date was set for the meetings during the dry season and Art made the trip. Less than a mile from the town there was a stream bed to cross. The banks had been cut down but it was still too steep for the pick-up. Going up the far side, the back bumper dragged in the dry sandy stream bed and the camper caught in the dirt. After Art got help, he finally arrived in Zamalo.

Sunday morning the services began. The people were hungry for the Word of God. When it was service time, work was laid aside and the Christians gathered expecting something from the Lord. God blessed in a gracious way and some of the Christians stayed for prayer help. One woman came for prayer on behalf of her husband. Both had accepted the Lord as their Savior but seemingly never understood the Christian way of life. She became a strong Christian, but her husband was being strongly influenced by some Moslems. Several came with their problems and burdens, seeking help and advice, desiring to draw closer to the Lord.

"I planned to return to Salka on Monday," Art said. "About eleven o'clock Sunday night a storm came up and it rained and rained. Monday night it rained again. The men worked cheerfully, digging out where the dirt had washed away so I could get out of town with the pick-up. About noon Tuesday we had the pick-up across the stream. When I had traveled the four miles back to the new road, I thought my trouble would be over; however I met an Italian man walking along the road. He said the wooden bridge across a small river had washed out, and most of their equipment was stuck in the mud. As I arrived at the site, I saw it was impossible for me to get across. What was I to do? God made a way for Moses to cross the Red Sea. Would he make a way for me?

The equipment belonging to the construction company was on the same side of the river that I was, and they also wanted to get across. They began pushing dirt into the river to fill it up and make a way across. By night I was able to get to Yelwa and then on home the next day. It took two and a half days to travel less than one hundred miles, but I arrived home praising the Lord for a wonderful week of fellowship with the Christians in Zamalo, for the spiritual victories that had been won and for making a way across the river when there was none.

FROM LOCAL BOY TO AMBASSADOR

When Gladys returned to the Bible School they had had Nigerian principals. Jacob Bawa had been one of these. He was a Salka boy who had received Christ as his Savior when he was a lad in primary school. He was raised in a pagan home. One day a friend of his invited him to go to church. A missionary preached from Romans 3:23 and through it the Lord spoke to Jacob but he did not receive Christ then. He returned to church the next Sunday and accepted Christ as his Savior. About a year after his conversion he went to a mission school to learn more about God and to prepare to become a teacher. One day a Nigerian pastor spoke on 'God's Call.' He said, "One day all the missionaries will go back to their countries and who will carry on the Lord's work in our land?" This message was a great challenge to him and he felt that God was telling him to go to a theological college, and after that he should go into the ministry.

Though he taught in a mission school, he had no peace because God's Spirit kept telling him that this was not the place God wanted him. He thought that if he were teaching in some other school, he would be happy. The government needed agricultural instructors so he applied and taught for the government. Still the Lord kept speaking to him, telling him to go to a Bible College. During revival services in one of the evangelical churches in his city, he rededicated his life to God and was willing to do what God wanted. After this he went to Ilorin Theological College and then was returned to his own tribe as pastor of the Salka Church and a teacher in the Hausa Bible School.

Later Jacob continued his education by attending college in the United States. He received his B.S. in Theology Degree at Emmanuel Bible College in Kitchener, Ontario, Canada; and his Master of Christian Education and Theology degrees at Trinity College. Eventually he graduated from Michigan State University with his Doctorate degree. When he returned to Nigeria, he was the first National President of the United Missionary Church of Africa (U.M.C.A.). God has continued to lead his life and today (1992) he is the Nigerian Ambassador to Spain. Jacob Bawa has come a long way from the backward-pagan village of Salka. As he obeyed God, the doors have opened before him throughout his life thus far.

GOD'S BLESSINGS CAME UNANNOUNCED

Through the pages of the *Missionary Banner* in 1967 Rev. John Moran told about one special day in the Salka Bible School. *For a week our class had discussed the work of the Holy Spirit in sanctification. As the period was drawing to a close, I concluded with an illustration of the work of the Holy Spirit in purifying the heart of the Christian and ruling in his heart without a rival. I closed my Bible and put away my notes. Instantly one of the young men stood to his feet to speak. "I know I have received this cleansing, but I feel I have allowed myself to drift. I do not sense God's presence as I once did. I want you to pray for me." Immediately God's presence became unusually real. As he sat down, one of the others stood. "I know I am a true Christian. My sins are forgiven," and he continued with a glowing testimony of his conversion. "But," he went on, "I have never been able to fully and completely consecrate myself to God as we have heard in this course. I want to pray now that God will help me give myself fully to Him. I want this purification."*

Six of these fine young men stood requesting that we pray for them. The Class was turned into a prayer meeting. I poured out my heart together with them that God would meet every single heart in cleansing power. Spontaneously they stood to their feet again, one by one, to give God praise for sanctifying their hearts. It was a blessed scene. Sometimes black faces shine better than white ones!

It is very evident that the need is great for sanctified, well-trained men, prepared in head and heart to become pastors in the northern villages of the U.M.C.A. To help in this preparation, the Salka Bible School is dedicated to help meet this need by teaching the Bible and its related subjects, providing practical village work, giving personal counsel and living a Christian life before them. However, none of these will take the place of the initial preparation which these six men received in their hearts last week. Without the purifying Spirit, all else is poor preparation indeed.

EYE TROUBLE

The children from Hillcrest School returned to their homes for summer vacation in June, 1968. Since there were quite a few U.M.S. children going to school at this time, some of the parents would go to Jos to bring them home. They had a platform, which was made to fit in the back of pick-ups, so the suitcases could be put under the platform. A mattress was put on top so the children could lie down or sit on it. Eva Mae and Elmer came home on a Thursday with the rest of the children. On the following Monday afternoon, Elmer began to complain about his eyes being watery. The next morning they were swollen shut and he could not see. I started putting eye drops into his eyes. One day after having family devotions and having prayed especially for Elmer's eyes, he began to cry and said, "I will never see again." His sister, Eva Mae, said, "Elmer, where is your faith?" We had just prayed and asked God to help his eyes get better, why not believe that

God would help him? One got better, but the other got
worse. On Saturday morning I noticed how strange that
eye looked, and we decided to take him to the doctor,
a trip of one hundred miles each way.

After examining Elmer's eye, Dr. Yates recommended taking him to the Government Hospital in
Ibadan immediately. Monday morning we were at the
hospital in Ibadan. The letter that Dr. Yates wrote to the
doctor was taken into the operating theatre where she
was operating when we arrived. As soon as possible she
came out and looked at Elmer's eye and started treatment even before he was admitted to the hospital. God
had truly opened the way for us to see the doctor.
Elmer's problem was diagnosed as deep-center kerati-
tis - cause unknown. For ten days the doctor did not
give any hope that they would be able to save his eye.
If it perforated they would have to remove it.

The West African Congress on Evangelism was
being held in Ibadan at that time. More than one
thousand people attending that meeting put Elmer on
their prayer lists and prayed for him several times a
day. God undertook and his eye healed. The scar
formed over the pupil of his eye so he could not see
with that eye but he had good vision in the other one. In
August Elmer went back to school with the other
children, but was taken to the eye hospital in Kano
several times during the school term. A visiting doctor
there suggested that Elmer be taken home for a cornea
transplant.

June, 1969, found us on our way home again after a
short term of two years. At times I had not been feeling
well either so, when we got home, Elmer had a cornea

transplant at Case Western Reserve Hospital in Cleveland and I had gall bladder surgery at the Cleveland Clinic. Art was kept busy with hospital visitation since we were in separate hospitals at the same time. One day my roommate said to Art, "At times like this, don't you feel like giving up your faith?" Art answered, "What would I do at a time like this, without my faith?"

After a year the doctors gave both Elmer and I permission to return to Nigeria. Elmer could still see with only one eye. He does have a little sight in it today, but it is very little and does not focus with his good eye. We are thankful that he has good vision in his left eye and he gets along very well.

ANOTHER WEDDING

Before we returned to Nigeria, Earl and Martha (Marty) Bradley were married. They lived near Dowagiac, Michigan, and pastored a small church. Earl had graduated from Bethel and Marty had two more years of school.

THE POISONER POISONED

During Bible School vacation I went to the villages with Art. One time we went to Senci for special services in the church. Among those who came for prayer were two women. The older woman was the mother-in-law of the younger woman but their problem was really one. The son of the older woman, and husband of the younger woman, was a soldier so he was not home much of the time. He had been a Christian at one time but was not walking with the Lord. He took a second wife and brought her home to live with his mother and first wife. Up until that time they had had a happy home and all had gone well. When the second wife came, there was much arguing and quarreling with no peace in the home. The mother and first wife stayed for prayer and sought help from the Lord during the meetings. They cried out to God for His help because they did not want all this arguing. They knew that it was not pleasing to the Lord, and was not a good testimony to others around them. They also prayed for Laraba's salvation. She had come to the meetings, but did not yield to the call to repentance. She was not happy either but she went on in her own way, and eventually made her plans without seeking any guidance from the Lord.

"Now I've got the poison," Laraba muttered to herself as she hurried home from the market. "It won't be long now. Soon no first wife and no mother-in-law! Then my problems will all be finished. The medicine man said it couldn't fail. I've waited so long for this that I . . ."

Her thoughts were suddenly interrupted by a sharp pain in her foot. "SNAKE!" she cried out in terror. "I've been bitten by a snake! Aiya! Aiya!"

Instead of going home as she planned, Laraba had to turn around and go back to the large town where she had bought the poison a few hours before. She had planned to poison her mother-in-law and the first wife, but now she went back to get an injection of snake serum to save her life. Two days later people were saying, "Laraba is dying of snake bite."

At this very time we were in the area after the Hausa Camp Meeting. Immediately after we arrived at the mission station in Zuru, we were told that a woman was dying in the dispensary. She had been bitten by a snake. Would we rush her to the hospital at Tungam Magajiya? It was twenty miles away, but perhaps the doctor there could save her life.

On the way to the T.M. Hospital, as we passed through the town where the Camp had been held, we were stopped by a pastor who said, "Please, my wife is in labor. Will you take her to the hospital?" Now we had two patients.

A few days later news of the two women reached us. "The pastor's wife has a healthy baby," they said, "but the woman who was bitten by a snake died. She was Laraba." We had not recognized her when we took her to the hospital. It had been about two weeks since her mother-in-law had prayed so earnestly for her salvation.

"But wait," we were told, "God did answer prayer." It seems that she went to see her husband and stayed a few days. While there she decided to get rid of her mother-in-law and the other wife. On her return home, she went to a medicine man in a small village to buy some poison. He promised to have it ready for her in four days and arranged to meet her in the market-place six miles from her home. There she bought the poison and was prepared to carry out her evil plan. On the way home from this secret meeting, she was bitten by the snake and never got to use the medicine.

How do we know all this? She herself told it just before she died. She called the pastor's wife who had been in the pick-up with her on the way to the hospital and asked her to help her find Christ. "I know I am going to die and I am not ready," she said. On her death bed she made this terrible confession and asked for forgiveness. How gracious and merciful the loving Savior is! Laraba's sinful heart was washed in Jesus' blood and Christ had taken her home to be with Him in heaven.

THE ACIFAWA TRIBE

Some of the national pastors had been telling Art about the Acifawa tribe. It was hard to believe what they were telling him but he wanted to find out the facts for himself. Later he made the trip with them to the top of the hill where their main town is located. They had to climb and climb through an area where no one could even see a path because it went over large rocks. Would it be worth this difficult trip to try to take the Gospel message to this tribe? As far as Art could determine, it had been eighteen years since any white man had visited the town.

When the small party of men arrived at the top of the hill, a big celebration was in progress. The old Chief had died and a new Chief was being installed. The people asked Art and the pastors, "What are you doing here?" They answered, "We have come to greet your Chief." They were taken to a little hut to wait while the men went to see if the Chief would see the visitors. While they waited for the men to return, some other people came into the hut to greet them. Art had taken a gramophone with him, so after the salutations were over they played Gospel recordings for them.

After a while the men returned and said that the Chief would see them now. They all got up to go but only two or three were allowed to go and the rest had to wait. At the Chief's entrance hut, they were again asked to wait. Soon Art was given permission to enter but the others were told to stay where they were. Art began to wonder what he had gotten into but he followed the men in to see the Chief. As he entered, he began to salute the Chief using the Hausa language. The men stopped him, saying, "You can not talk directly to him. He is so great." Art spoke in Hausa and the men translated into the Acifawa language although the Chief had understood what Art was saying.

Usually when someone visits this Chief, a man stands behind him waving his hands back and forth over him repeating, "There is no difference between our Chief and God. Our Chief is the same as God," all the time the visitor is there. However this day they did not do that. It may have been because he was a new Chief just being installed. The day Art saw him the new Chief was not blind but he understood that their Chiefs had been blind for generations. Art was told that, before the Chief was installed, he had to agree to become blind. This was accomplished by the Chief leaning over a fire containing a certain substance which caused blindness. The next time Art saw him he was nearly blind.

Art shared the Gospel with him and his men. The second time he went to see him, they did carry on the ritual of waving their hands over him and saying, "There is no difference between our Chief and God." They did hear the Gospel story though and, when Art and his party left the Chief's hut, one of the elders got up and followed them down the path. He called to them and asked if this salvation would be good for him too.

The men sat down by the path and led this elderly man to the Lord, and then went on their way. The pastor from a nearby village kept in contact with him and helped him follow in the Christian way. As far as we know, three from this tribe have become Christians. This elderly man passed away a few months after his conversion.

A doctor at the T.M. Hospital became interested in this tribe because of a patient who had come to the hospital. Arrangements were made and he visited them. While there, he examined the Chief's eyes. A short time later, Art and some others planned to go again. Art got sick and could not go but he asked them to greet the Chief for him. When they did so, thinking it was the doctor who sent greetings, he said, "When you get back to the doctor, will you ask him if he will come again and do something about my sight?" By that time he had realized what he had given up for the honor of being Chief.

One of the Agwara pastors had heard about this tribe and wondered why the missionary and others were so compelled to make the difficult climb to reach this village. He prayed, saying to the Lord, "Lord, I want you to show me what these other men see and feel as they visit this tribe." When another group made the trip, he went along. Afterwards he said to Art, "God has shown me what you have seen. I am going back to my church to get some of the Christians to help me reach the Acifawa." This was a real encouragement to Art. Our furlough was nearly due again, and he wanted someone to take the responsibility of continuing to reach this group of people for Christ. However, while we were in America we received a letter telling us that Pastor Shirika had passed away - the one pastor who was really carrying a burden for the Acifawa people. Since that time others have gone occasionally, but there has been no regular contact with these who are still spiritually blind and need the Savior.

RETURNING AFTER FURLOUGH

Eva Mae graduated from Goshen High School in June, 1975. We left for Nigeria a few weeks after her graduation. It was difficult to leave her. In fact, it was like taking a sheet and tearing it in half. She seemed happy with the plans that had been made concerning her future and was willing for us to go, even if it was a difficult time to say goodbye.

Elmer also had a struggle - not only because of leaving his brother and sisters behind, but also because of Bicentennial preparations being made in the United States for 1976. He did not want to leave America at this important historical celebration.

We had received our re-entry permits in Nigeria which were valid for one year before we came home in the summer of 1974. If time ran out, it would be impossible to get return visas because none were being issued at that time. We felt that God was urging us on. So, with the knowledge that we were in God's will, we proceeded to plan our return.

During our furlough we had been receiving letters from some Christians in Salka indicating that something was happening in the town. Since there were no missionaries there, we were glad for the letters, but the information we received made it impossible to piece together what was taking place.

After attending the Camp Meeting in Salka, Lois Fuller wrote a thrilling account of what was taking place in Salka. Lois' article was entitled, *Two Hundred and Fifty Converts at Salka, Nigeria:*

Missionary Church missionaries to Nigeria have been talking about Salka a lot lately. I spent ten days there this spring with Rev. Jacob Bawa and a team of ten students from the Theological College. As a native of the town, Rev. Bawa really understood the significance of recent events there, and I want to try to explain them to you as he explained them to me.

The town is organized in five sections based on family groups. Before December, 1974, all five of these sections officially supported the pagan Magiro worship. There are also some Muslims in town and, of course, our missionaries have been there for many years - the fruits of their labors being the church and the Hausa Bible School.

Magiro consists of the spirits of the dead. When a woman hears the strange piping noise of Magiro coming toward her compound at night, she must quickly run and barricade herself in her hut, lest it should kill her. The men tell her if its strange piping had a message for her. She must do what these spirits say or she knows she will likely die - be killed, as she believes by Magiro.

It is different for the men. At the age of ten or twelve, a boy is initiated into the mysteries of Magiro. He is shown the flute that the men play to make the piping noise. And he is threatened with death if he should tell any woman, even his mother, the source of this sound. Despite the deception involved, Kamberi men really do believe that there is spiritual power behind the worship. Sacrifices must be made to the Magiro spirits and the flute purified with blood. The blood of chickens is put on the doorposts of houses and food offerings are left out on certain nights for the Magiro spirits to eat. Although the men who do the piping eat these, they believe they are doing it for Magiro. They think of Magiro as a mediator between the High God and living man. Every December, Magiro worshippers (men only) join for a seven-day festival. The women stay inside their homes in fear.

Before last year's festival, the head blacksmith in Salka had died. It is an honor for a blacksmith to be crowned as head of all the other blacksmiths in town. Usually the privilege is rotated among the five sections of town. This time the head blacksmith should be chosen from a certain section called Ketarin Daji.

The Chief of Salka and his council, however, chose a man from the same section as the man who had just died. The people of Ketarin Daji were furious. They told the Chief they were pulling out of Salka, rejecting him, and setting up their own Chief to rule them independently.

When the time for the Magiro festival came, most of the men from Ketarin Daji boycotted the festivities. But about ten men, against the advice of their friends, decided to go. When they arrived, the men from the other sections of town challenged them, "What are you doing here? We thought you said you didn't want to belong with us any more." The men replied, "We want to have our share in Magiro too." At that the men from the rest of the town ganged up on the men from Ketarin

*Daji and one was killed. The survivors reported what
had happened at the feast and the men of Ketarin Daji,
armed with guns, bows and axes came against the men
who had done the deed. After more fighting, peace was
finally restored by the local government authorities.
But the men from Ketarin Daji were thoroughly fed up
with Magiro. They brought out the flutes and explained
everything to the women. They declared they would
have no more to do with pagan worship.*

*There is another kind of pagan worship in Salka
called Agunu. After this trouble over Magiro, another
section of town pulled out of the Agunu cult and
declared that they, too, had given up pagan worship.
Members of the Agunu cult are supposed to be very
loyal to each other, but a young man from the family of
the cult leader himself had stolen the fiancee of another
Agunu member. The section to which the wronged man
belonged said that this proved that Agunu was not a
true religion, so they left the cult.*

*All of these events left a tremendous spiritual vac-
uum in the town. Some Muslims attempted to get those
who had given up paganism to turn to Islam instead.
But the Christians saw the opportunity too and knew
God's hand was working to bring the people of Salka to
Himself. Many of the ex-pagans began searching for
the spiritual life they had seen among Christians in the
town. "Pasto, Pasto, will you help us find the Jesus
way?" cried a number of men who had searched the
town for Pastor Ibrahim.*

*Some came to the church services and accepted
Christ there. Others sought out Christian friends and
neighbors to ask the way of salvation. As the Christians*

witnessed to these hungry people, more and more came until, by the first week of March when our team from the college arrived in Salka, there were about one hundred twenty new converts.

Anyone could see that this was going to present some real challenges to the church in Salka. The present church building holds only about two hundred people. Dozens of new Christians need to be taught the disciplines of the Christian life.

On the last night of the camp meeting, Rev. Bawa preached a stirring message aimed at the Christians. The congregation contained several Bible School graduates now in private business and other capable Christians who had neglected the spiritual ministries for which God had fitted them. At the invitation, about twenty of these men stood to publicly dedicate themselves to this great task of carrying on what God is doing there.

The same issue of the *Missionary Banner* that ran Lois's article also printed our farewell letter to friends at home. In our letter we had written:

It has been reported that two hundred to three hundred Kamberi people from Salka have come to the Lord during this past year. Our hearts are thrilled by this report but we know that there is a terrific battle going on. The devil is very displeased. He will do his best to get some of them to fall back, and to keep others from repenting of their sins; but we are looking to God for real victory and for a great awakening, not only in Salka but among the whole Kamberi tribe.

When we went home in June, 1974, there were about two hundred fifty attending the church. When we arrived back one year later, there were about six hundred. As we heard the story of what happened in our absence, we realized how God had kept his promise, ''So shall my word be that goeth forth out of my mouth: it shall not return unto me void, but it shall accomplish that which I please, and it shall prosper in the thing whereto I sent it'' (Isaiah 55:11). His word had been sown for many, many years in Salka. Little by little there was fruit, but now God used the fight among the fetish members to remind the Kamberi of the seed of God's Word that had been planted in the hearts of many of them through the years and a harvest has been reaped. The church continues to grow.

A NEW CHURCH

After a few months, the church board members told Art they had decided to build a new church since the Christians could not all get into the church for services. They wanted to build a solid building with cement blocks, a corrugated iron roof and a cement floor. What would it cost for such a building? At first Art tried to persuade them to build with mud blocks and plaster it with cement. It would be much less expensive as they could make the blocks themselves, and it would be durable. He knew that the average annual wage in Nigeria at the time was about three hundred dollars, but they were determined to build a cement block building which would last a long time. They figured that eighty feet by thirty feet would be large enough.

After getting the price of materials, the board was told that it would cost approximately ten thousand dollars. They said they would do it. The next Sunday it was announced in church what the building would cost. The people were told to go home and pray about it. Three weeks later, the pastor said that now they should pray that God would show each of them how much money they should give to the building fund the next Sunday.

When the offering was taken the next Sunday they had enough to begin the foundation. A contractor came and laid the foundation. There was some money left so the cement blocks were started. When the money was gone the contractor went home and the people started to pray again. The church was built by prayer and obedience to God. It was a miracle to see the church go up little by little, being paid for as they built. Eventually they decided they wanted to be worshiping in the new church for the Christmas service in 1977, so they worked and prayed with that goal in mind, saying they would do it even if they had to sit on a dirt floor.

During this time we received a letter from a friend in America who asked us if we were involved in some project where we could use two thousand dollars that would be given as a memorial on behalf of her parents who had both passed on to their eternal reward. They had always been keenly interested in the mission work in Nigeria, and had prayed fervently for that work. Art had not mentioned this sum of money to the church board because we did not know what red tape might be involved or when the money might come. When it came, he called the board together and told them that we had received two thousand dollars from friends in America to help finish their church building. There was a real prayer meeting of thanksgiving and praise that evening. One of the board members said that they had prayed and prayed. They had brought what they could but there was no more to bring. They could see no possible way to get the rest of the money to finish the church. They had given eight thousand dollars and now God had provided the rest.

On Christmas Day, 1977, there were one thousand two hundred and ninety four people by actual count that tried to squeeze into the new building for the first service. Although there were no seats, they brought the benches from the old church and stools, chairs, and mats to sit on and worshiped the Lord Jesus Christ who was their Savior. The church was not large enough for the first service and has not been big enough since. In a period of five Sundays surrounding the Christmas season, a total of two hundred more people came forward and accepted Jesus as their personal Savior.

The church was completed with wooden seats and was dedicated in April, 1978. The church has grown more slowly recently than in those first two years but two more churches have been built in different sections of the town.

NIGERIA - A SUCCESS STORY

There are three chapters to the history of the Church in Nigeria thus far. The early years of the twentieth century, when Rev. A. W. Banfield and his party traveled up the Niger River to a town called Shonga marked the beginning of the Missionary Church work in Nigeria. From that early start the work began to expand to the south in Yoruba area, through the central part in Nupe area, and in the north through the Hausa area.

The missionary was the complete authority in the beginning. Everything hinged on what he did and said. He started the schools and taught them. He preached and God gave the increase. As the light of Christianity dawned, and in order to prepare the local people to assume leadership in their churches, schools were started and became a significant part of the educational development of the country. Bible classes in the schools were a daily part of the curriculum and many of the students came to know Christ as their Savior. The first fifty years of missionary work saw the development of institutions to train teachers for the schools, Bible Schools to train pastors for the churches, and practical training for medical work in the dispensaries.

The second chapter of the history of the Nigerian Church began in 1955 when the United Missionary Church of Africa (U.M.C.A.) was organized and a constitution was written. Nationals became leaders of the church as well as pastors of local congregations. A joint council was formed with the missionaries and nationals counseling together. Nationals were teaching in the schools, working in the dispensaries, giving suggestions and helping decide church policy. Missionaries and nationals were sharing and laboring side by side, working together with God to build His church in Nigeria. A partnership was developed and maintained between the missionary and the national church.

The third chapter of the history began in January, 1978, when the nationals took over full responsibility and authority in the Church. Missionaries worked under the authority of the nationals. Today the national church leads and the missionary assists.

Six months after the 'Handing Over Service' when the mission handed over the responsibilities of the church to the national church, we came home. My burden and question to the congregations and individuals to whom I spoke while on furlough was, "How will this third chapter of the history of the Nigerian Church be written if it depends on your prayers? Will it be one of victory, rapid growth, a strong church; or will it be a defeated, weak church, struggling to stay in existence?"

Praise God for the faithful intercessors who have prayed. The work has grown rapidly and His church in Nigeria is thriving. God's power never fails so let us move the hand of God by our prayers that He will give constant victory to His children and His church in Nigeria.

FURLOUGH AND A LEAVE OF ABSENCE

As we planned to return home for furlough again, we were not sure of God's leading for the future. Elmer would be graduating from high school in Jos and he did not know what he wanted to do, except that he did not want to go to college. As he anticipated coming to the States, he felt he did not even know his own relatives. So he asked Mom and Dad to stick with him. We felt he was our responsibility and that the next two or three years would be a critical time in his life.

After our year of furlough we asked the Mission Board for a leave of absence. Art worked for Bethel Publishing Company in Elkhart, Indiana, and I worked at Hubbard Hill Retirement Center in the nursing wing.

Elmer took some vocational training in woodworking and construction and got a job in that line of work. God had a plan for Elmer's life but Elmer did not know what it was.

The time came when Elmer knew he must let go of Mom and Dad and he freed us to our call. One day after his struggle was settled in his own heart and mind, although he did not know what the future held for him, he said to us, "Mom and Dad, you can go back to Nigeria now if you want to." We did not know of the struggle that he had been through at the time, but we knew that God was working in his life. A short time later, as Elmer was listening to his father sharing a message which he had heard a number of times before, God spoke to him and asked him to be a missionary and share God's message of love with the people of Sierra Leone, West Africa.

After Elmer heard the call of God, he decided to go to Emmanuel Bible College in Kitchener, Ontario, the following fall. We began making plans to return to Nigeria but it was not God's time yet for us to do so. Through that winter Art would occasionally have slight pains across his chest. Although we went to the doctor at different times, no reason for them had been found. We had appointments for physical check-ups the day after Easter. The doctor wanted Art to see a specialist about his problem. On Good Friday he went and was told he had angina. We asked for another extension of our leave of absence to give us time to have it taken care of. For a while there were doubts in our minds if we would ever get back to Nigeria but, after by-pass surgery and a complete and speedy recovery, the doctor at Cleveland Clinic gave his approval for Art to return to Africa.

After Art's recovery, we were both questioned closely by the Mission Board about our desire to return. The Board reminded us that if we returned to Africa, there were no medical facilities where we could get any immediate help. Did we really want to go back under those conditions? Art answered that it was no farther from Nigeria to heaven than it is from America to heaven. We were allowed to return.

In July, 1983, we were on our way back to the land of our calling. I would be teaching in the Bible School again and Art was asked to help open an area to the Gospel which had become a great concern to the national church as well as the missionaries.

THE TRIANGLE

The people in this region represent a tribe inhabiting approximately thirteen hundred square miles between Yelwa, Kontagora, and Tungam Magajiya. They were essentially untouched by the Gospel message. The very remote area was entirely bush. The people lived in little hamlets scattered all through the territory.

Some years ago one of our missionaries cycled through this vast bush country to preach and survey the area. From that day to the present, very little work was done in this interior region. The extent of any witnessing accomplished had been along the edges of the triangle formed by the location of the three mission stations mentioned.

Art prayed and wondered how to begin working in this tract known as 'The Triangle.' Finally he asked

Pastor Phillip from Yelwa if he would go along and help him. Pastor Phillip inquired about the area by asking some policemen in his church for information. He was told that at Tungam Bunu, where there was a U.M.C.A. church, there was a road back into Dan Maraya. If they went there, they would find lots of people.

After making arrangements to go to Dan Maraya, Art picked Pastor Phillip up at Yelwa and they set off. The bush road was not very good and it took them about four hours to travel twenty-two miles. As soon as they arrived, they were surrounded by curious people many of whom had never seen a white man. Art and Pastor Phillip said they had come to bring a message to the people of their area and they were interested in becoming acquainted.

According to the townspeople, the next day was market day when many people from the hamlets and small villages would be coming into town. The men parked the pick-up and stayed overnight.

The next morning when some young Kamberi men came along the path, Art and Pastor Phillip invited them over to hear a message. They visited in the Hausa language, then played a cassette tape in their dialect of the Kamberi language. The young men were excited to hear the tape in their own dialect. Art and Pastor Phillip said to the young men, "We do not understand your dialect so would you tell us in Hausa what you just heard in your language?" They did this and then had the opportunity to ask questions. Those young men went on to market. They were told that Pastor Phillip and the Bature (white man) would be visiting their villages and compounds within the next few days.

Soon another group of people came and said, "We hear that you have something that talks in our language. Can we hear it too?" Again they played the tape and had them tell what they understood, then answered their questions. This went on all day long. One group would follow another.

The next day Art and Pastor Phillip began to walk. Dan Maraya was at the end of the motor road so any place they went from there was by foot. They walked in one direction stopping at all the hamlets they saw and playing the gospel recording tape. The next day they walked in another direction doing the same thing until they had covered much of the area around Dan Maraya.

The question could be raised as to why they did not gather the people together and preach to them. Why did they just play the tape? First, tapes were in the language of the people. Second, at that time it was illegal to hold an open air service. There had been some trouble in Nigeria, and an edict was issued that no open air services were allowed. Moslems were to gather in their Mosques and Christians were to gather in their churches. Art and his helpers were not disobeying the law when they simply played the tapes and then visited with the people, answering their questions in the course of conversation. They had no trouble.

When Art and Pastor Phillip returned from each day's trek, Art would come back with a heavy heart, asking God, "When will they hear the message of salvation?" Among all the people he met on these first trips to the area, only one elderly man said, "I have heard this story before." The elderly man said that one time many years ago there was an epidemic spreading in their village and they needed medicine to stop it. After inquiries they were told that at Yelwa, about a forty mile walk through the bush, there was a white lady who had medicine that might help them. He was one of those chosen to go to Yelwa. When they got there they were directed to the Mission compound where Matar Mallam (Mrs. Earl Honsberger) was doing dispensary work. Every morning before she gave out medicine, she told the patients the story of Jesus. This man had not accepted Jesus but he remembered having heard about Him. Only one out of so many had ever heard the gospel message before!

In one town a few young men wanted to follow the Jesus way. They needed to be taught what it meant to follow Jesus, how to worship Him, and how to read His word and pray.

One of the graduates from the Salka Bible School was stationed in Tungam Bunu on the edge of the triangle. Art and Pastor Phillip took him to some of the villages and introduced him to the young men who wanted to follow Jesus. He began walking out, about eighteen miles each trip, every other day to have prayer with them, teach them songs and teach them to read.

Many trips were made into the area, many Christians, pastors, students and evangelists helped get the work started. One time the Gospel Team from Salka (about sixty in number) left early on a Sunday morning. They loaded up three small pick-ups and traveled about eighty miles to Dan Maraya. When they arrived they divided into groups and walked to many hamlets all day to tell the people about Jesus and His love for them. It was after dark when they returned home. As they came into town they were singing and praising God. Later we heard they had prayed with more than forty people and led them to Christ. This was cause for great rejoicing. The need to disciple these new converts was real. They had no Bibles and could not read anyway. Pastors were needed to live in the area so they could teach the people. There were not enough pastors but Pastor Wana Gero from Tungam Bunu kept in contact with them and encouraged some to go to Bible School later.

TUNGAM MAGAJI

The Gospel Team from Yelwa had been going out near the old airport in Yelwa to hold services on Sunday afternoons. One day during a service, a woman from a nearby town was going through the town on her way home from market. She heard singing and stopped to find its source. She heard a wonderful story of love. After that she often made it a point to be in that village about the same time, so she could hear more about the One who loved everyone so much that He gave His life for them. Finally she accepted this Jesus she had been hearing about and asked Him to forgive her sins. She went home and tried to tell her people about Jesus, but they would not listen to her. They said she was a witch and did not know what she was talking about. Nearly two years after her conversion, a young man from her town decided to go to Salka to visit a friend. He arrived in Salka on Friday intending to stay only for market on Saturday but his friend, who had become a Christian, persuaded him to stay and attend church on Sunday. He was told that he would see a lot of Kamberi who were following the Jesus way. That Sunday he gave his heart to the Lord. On Monday he went back home and told his people that what that woman was trying to tell them about Jesus was the truth. He explained that there were a lot of Kamberi in Salka following the Lord Jesus and that he, too had accepted Jesus as his Savior while in Salka.

This happened at the time the Yelwa Camp Meeting was to start. Sunday morning someone brought the pastor a scrap of paper. The note asked him to come to a certain village because the people there wanted to repent and turn to Jesus. Pastor Phillip was not sure where this village was located. He had never received a request like this before in all the years of his ministry. What did this mean?

On Sunday afternoon he and the Gospel Team set out to find this village. When they arrived they found that most of the people from that first Christian lady's compound wanted to accept Christ. There were about forty people who came to Jesus that day seeking a new life in Christ. The people had seen a change in that woman's life but had not paid attention to the reason for the change when she tried to tell them. When the young man also came back as a Christian, they listened and wanted the happiness he had found. Some of the people came to camp meeting to hear more about Jesus. After camp was over, Art, Pastor Phillip and Rev. Naduku spent a few days in their village. More people repented and chose to follow Jesus. In due time a pastor was stationed in the village. The people continued to follow the Lord. One day they called Pastor Phillip to come and help them burn or destroy the instruments of the fetish worship in their town. They earnestly wanted to follow Jesus.

FAREWELL TO THE REIFELS

As the time for our retirement drew near, we had mixed feelings about some of the farewell gatherings that were planned. The first one was held in Zuru at the pastors' monthly meeting. I had taught most of the pastors in Bible School and Art had worked with most of them in their churches and in village work. Art had become known as *Baturen Daji (White Man of the Bush)* because of all the time he spent in the villages to help plant churches and to strengthen those already established.

At the Bible School in Salka we had a farewell dinner with the students and their families and some of the school board members. There were also farewells by the Women's group and the entire church. Several outfits of national clothing were presented to us. Group pictures were taken so we could remember those of our children in the Lord, and those we had taught and worked with. There were tears shed, both by the nationals and by us as the time came for us to part. We were not expecting to see one another again until we meet in our heavenly home. It is always difficult to sing the song, "God be with you 'til we meet again" at such a time but truly that was their prayer and ours as we joined together in singing the song in Hausa, expecting to see each other again when God calls His prepared and faithful followers home.

EPILOGUE AND FAMILY MEMORIES

Art and I retired from Missionary service in June, 1988. We give God the praise for allowing us many years in His service in Nigeria, and for those who have been raised up among the Nationals to continue the work. Truly He is a faithful God who is able to do abundantly above what is asked of Him.

We have traveled in deputation work in all the Districts of the Missionary Church in the United States and Canada except Hawaii, speaking in churches, challenging God's people to pray that His kingdom might be extended in Nigeria.

We are now living in Mishawaka, Indiana, doing visitation work for the Bethany Missionary Church of Elkhart. I am also Prayer Chairman for the Missionary Women International of the North Central District of the Missionary Church.

CONNIE

Connie, the oldest of the Reifel children, remained in the States at the age of sixteen. She lived with my sister, Lila Adams, and her daughter, Sharon, who accepted her into their family. From the time she was a junior in high school, she remained in the United States in order to further her education. After two years at Bethel College in Mishawaka, Indiana, she married and continued her education at Emmanuel Bible College in Kitchener, Ontario, as well as being a pastor's wife. Later, when difficulties hit her life, only the strong faith instilled by her upbringing and the support of her parents carried her through. Though miles separated the family and she knew her parents were very disappointed, she also knew that they would not love her any less, which she found to be an outstanding example of love in action. She found that example to be very helpful in raising her own children.

Connie later married Keith Gary and, pressing forward, she did not carry the baggage of bitterness. She has had the privilege of playing the organ or pipe organ in many churches over the years. At present she is the Music Director and Pipe Organist for the historic St. Paul's Methodist Church in South Bend, Indiana, which was begun by the late Clement Studebaker of the Studebaker Car Foundation.

Connie and Keith have raised five children. She often wondered if she would be able to relate to her own children due to having been raised in such a different environment. She discovered that those Boarding School rules work well when one has several children and now also grandchildren.

Was she deprived because of being brought up as an M.K. (Missionary's Kid)? Connie says, "No." She feels that since God called her parents to be missionaries, she was in that plan too, including being raised in a foreign land. She insists that most people have two obvious dimensions to themselves - a front and back. However, M.K.s have a third dimension that sometimes gets in the way - a totally different kind of facet that most people don't have, and can't see, and don't understand. She has concluded very emphatically that no one should hide that facet, because M.K.s are very special people and have a lot to give. She has been active in encouraging and supporting other M.K.s and in organizing get-togethers for M.K.s and their families.

Connie and her husband own a business as well as a shop called Connie's Corner, which is a floral, wedding and gift shop. Her interest in flowers was sparked by the British influence in gardens in Nigeria and while visiting England during the family travels. She appreciated the beauty of flowers and wildlife, and is presently the District Director of the North Central District Garden Clubs of Indiana.

EARL

During his senior year at Bethel College, Earl became the pastor of a small church in southwestern Michigan. A week after graduation, he married Martha Bradley and they settled into the parsonage where they began three years of church-extension ministry. It was an exciting and challenging time for them as they learned and grew together. Marty continued her education forty miles from their home. When Marty was a senior, God blessed their home with a little girl named Faith. Shortly after Marty's graduation they moved to the Detroit area to take a pastorate closer to Missionary Internship where their training for overseas service would begin.

Having completed the requirements for overseas service, Earl and Marty applied for missionary work in Nigeria. Unable to get visas at that time, they were encouraged to apply for visas to Sierra Leone. Their ministry in Sierra Leone has been primarily in evangelism and church planting since they arrived in the country in 1975.

Their three children, Faith, Toby and Andy, have

had most of their schooling experiences in a boarding school for missionaries' children where they have built deep and lasting friendships. They share with their parents the vision and excitement of reaching the Kuranko people with the Gospel and help in that effort whenever they can.

EVA MAE

Eva Mae is now living in South Bend, Indiana. She is married to Dennis Lanning and they have two children. Sara is in junior high and Christopher is in second grade. Eva Mae is working as a Patient Care Assistant at Memorial Hospital in South Bend and is attending school to receive her Associate Degree in Nursing.

Eva Mae feels that the greatest hardship that missionaries go through is the separation of leaving parents, family, and a familiar culture and venturing out into the unknown. To her, the family was very important and close knit. She says, "We enjoyed going out on evangelism trips when we were home on holiday, and the fact that four of us were crowded in a tiny pick-up camper did not seem to matter - we were doing it together."

As a missionary kid Eva Mae feels that if she had a choice and were to do it all over, she would not change being an M.K. She had a chance to see and do many things that most people will never experience. The only negative aspect she felt was the separation from family. In looking back, she feels that the positive outweighs the negative.

ELMER

Elmer also went to Hillcrest School in Jos, about four hundred miles from where we lived. He graduated in 1978 and we came home for furlough right after his graduation. We had lived in different areas of Michigan or Indiana every furlough since he had been born and he did not feel that he even knew his relatives, let alone have any close friends. So the thought of being left on his own in the States was more than he wanted to encounter. Not knowing what he wanted to do in life, he asked Mom and Dad to stay with him for a while. After our furlough was over, we took a leave of absence to stay home longer.

Elmer took a course in woodworking and got a job in construction. Later, in a service in which his Dad was preaching, he felt God's call to go as a missionary to Sierra Leone, West Africa. In answer to God's call, the following fall he went to Kitchener, Ontario, to attend Emmanuel Bible College.

While there he met Joann Grove and after graduation they were married. Elmer became the pastor at Wheatland Missionary Church in Michigan. They served at that church for four years and are now missionaries in Sierra Leone, West Africa.

Elmer and Joann have two children, Karalee and Kevan. When they left for Africa, Karalee was three years old and Kevan was two months old.

Through the years we were often asked if we wanted our children to be missionaries. Our answer was, "Only if God wants them to be." We want them to walk in the center of God's will so that He can make them a blessing and use them to help bring the lost to Him.

RETURN ON INVESTMENT
by
Rene Fretz and Michael Reynolds
Emphasis Magazine, 1987

There were sixty thousand people in the tribe, but only four Christians. Two of them, a husband and wife, lived in another town. The third was a leper who was so physically disabled he could not walk. The last was a young man who did some preaching and conducted services in a small church.

This is what Gladys and Art Reifel found during their first days as missionaries in Salka, Nigeria, back in 1945. In 1986, things are different and primarily because of the ministry of this couple.

Two hundred people were baptized at the 1986 Salka Camp Meeting. The little Salka church now averages over one thousand in attendance. In practically every village surrounding Salka there are groups of Christians, and some congregations as large as two hundred. When people give to World Missions, they want to know what they are receiving for their money. How is the church growing? How many souls have come to Christ? Gladys and Art Reifel and their ministry in Nigeria illustrate the importance of investing funds in effective missionaries. True missionaries are not those who go to a mission field to be a missionary. They are people who move into another country, and become a part of the culture and the people, so that some might be saved.

The commitment and energy given in ministry by the Reifels is seen in the names given to Art by Nigerians. Missionaries are often given African names because North American names seem hard for them to pronounce. His first name was one meaning 'Head of the House' and it was used until his fifth year on the field. Then a Chief from a small village decided Art needed a new name. "You work so hard going from village to village telling the Kamberi people the story of Jesus," said the Chief. "The Kamberi people really belong to you." The Chief gave Art a name which means 'Inheritor of the Kamberi Tribe.' As time went on, Art was given another name which means 'White Man of the Bush.' This fit because he spent so much time in remote villages.

Sending missionaries to the field is a large responsibility for the Missionary Church. We are not simply sending out a visitation team. We are sending people to confront and perhaps suffer the evil realities of Satan and the world.

One situation which threatened Art and Gladys followed the baptism of the first six converts from the Kamberi tribe. One of the baptized young men was preaching in the Salka church one Sunday morning. It was the time of year when leaders of the fetish, the superstitious religion of the country people, instructed all the women to make certain food for use in the fetish ritual.

The young preacher commented on Sunday that God gave us food and that, "We don't need to bring our bean cakes to God,'' or make an offering of these things to Him. The next day fifty or sixty men came storming up to the Reifels' home, talking to each other in loud, angry voices. They were upset about this preaching. Art and Gladys were scared.

Art talked with them. He explained that in the years they had lived in Salka, no missionary had spied on the fetish rituals or tried to rile up the people against their religion. After some time, the men agreed with Art and the crowd dispersed. Yet, many of the adults refused to let their children go to the evening classes conducted by Art and Gladys. They did not want their children to learn about the missionaries' God.

Everywhere you turn in the Salka area, you find the impact of the Missionary Church through the Reifels. We rejoice in their ministry and appreciate the return they bring to the Kingdom of God and to our investment in them.